PLAYBOY'S
GUIDE TO CASINO GAMBLING
Volume One: Craps

PLAYBOY'S
GUIDE TO
CASINO GAMBLING

Edwin Silberstang

Volume One: Craps

A PERIGEE BOOK

For Leslie and Philip

Perigee Books
are published by
The Putnam Publishing Group
200 Madison Avenue
New York, New York 10016

Library of Congress Cataloging in Publication Data

Silberstang, Edwin, date.

  Craps.
  (His Playboy's guide to casino gambling; v. 1)
  1. Craps (Game) I. Title. II. Series.
GV1303.s55 795.1 80-82971
ISBN 0-399-50948-8

First Perigee printing, 1983
Six previous Wideview printings
Printed in the United States of America
  2 3 4 5 6 7 8 9

CONTENTS

v

Contents

Contents

PLAYBOY'S
GUIDE TO CASINO GAMBLING
Volume One: Craps

INTRODUCTION

Craps is the fastest moving and most action packed of all casino games. It has the most vocal enthusiasts and while the other games are conducted in a sedate atmosphere, the craps table explodes with noise. The reason for this is obvious. Craps is far and away the most exciting casino game, where payoffs ride on every throw of the dice, where a $5 player can turn into a $100 bettor, where someone bringing $500 to the table can leave in an hour with $15,000. Craps is the type of game where money can be won in a hurry, if the dice are favorable to you.

The game has its pitfalls as well. Many bets are available on the craps layout, and a number of them are poor bets for the player, giving the house too much of an advantage. And since the game *is* so swift, a player can lose his or her head and make poor bets or play in such a manner as to minimize the chances of getting away a big winner.

Playboy's Guide to Casino Gambling: Craps has been written with all the above in mind. This book will show you not only how the game works and what bets are available, but also all bets will be carefully discussed and analyzed to show which are the soundest. In addition, the free-odds bets—the best ones the player can make—are fully covered. Not only will you fully understand the game after reading this book, but you will know the best betting methods available to take full advantage of what the game offers. Following these methods will minimize your risks and losses and maximize and enhance your profits.

The whole game of casino craps is covered in this book,

3

from the basic game all the way through proper money management. A chapter is devoted to the casino personnel staffing the table and running the game, including a discussion of proper tipping procedures for the dealers. Everything covered here will help to make you a winner, and by the time you finish this book, you'll know all you have to about this game to make it even more exciting than it is. For you'll be armed with inside facts and knowledge, and when you're at the craps table in a casino, making your intelligent wagers and handling your bets in the proper way, you'll get even more pleasure from the fact that this knowledge will enable you to win. There's nothing sweeter than winning, especially at an exciting game like craps.

I

CASINO PERSONNEL

THE CREW OF DEALERS

The dealers are the men and women with whom the bettors have the most contact, for these people run the actual game, handle the players' bets, collect and pay off wagers, and answer the gamblers' questions.

A crew at the craps table is made up of four individuals, but only three deal the game at any one time. The crew members alternate their duties, and each dealer has a twenty-minute "break" for every hour of dealing at the table. While one dealer is on break the other three are working at the table, dressed in the uniforms of the casino.

One dealer is designated the "stickman" or "on the stick" because this dealer uses a flexible stick to move the dice around the table. The other two dealers stand on the other side of the table, facing the stickman. These two dealers are "on base," and it is these men and women the players come in direct contact with and deal with throughout their play.

An additional casino employee, seated at the table between the two dealers on base, is known as the "boxman." Unlike the dealers in uniform, the boxman is dressed in either a suit or a sports jacket, and is considered an executive of the casino. His duties will be discussed later.

The Stickman

The dealer "on the stick," unlike the two standing dealers, doesn't usually deal directly with the players, but with the dice, for they are under his province and control.

At the onset of play, when a new shooter is "coming out," the stickman empties the small box or bowl of dice located in front of him and, with the stick, pushes the dice to the shooter. The shooter then selects two of the dice to roll, and the stickman pulls back the remaining dice and returns them to the box.

The shooter rolls the dice and after each roll, the stickman calls out the number rolled so that all players at the table know exactly what number has been thrown. Not only does the stickman call out the number rolled but he may give information about it. If a 7 was rolled on the come out, the stickman might say "Seven, a winner on the pass line, pay the front line." Or, if the established point was repeated and won, the stickman announces "The shooter made his point, pay the front line." However, should the shooter roll a 7 after the point was established, losing the roll, the stickman calls "Seven, line away, six was," the 6 referring to the point established.

After each roll of the dice, the stickman brings the dice back in front of him, while the dealers collect losing bets and pay off winning ones. Only after the dealers have finished does the stickman return the dice to the shooter.

The center, or proposition, bets are under the stickman's domain. The stickman places all bets thrown or given to him in the correct betting box on the center of the layout. These bets include hardways, any seven, any craps, and other proposition wagers, and will be discussed later. If the center bets lose, the stickman picks up the losing chips and gives them to the boxman. If the bets win, the stickman directs the dealers to pay off the winning players.

The stickman controls the tempo of the game, and often creates a lively and exciting game with his patter, "talking up" the game. He may exhort the players before the come-out roll to "bet craps, eleven, bet the field, get that money down on any craps." During the course of a roll, he might ask the players to "bet the come, bet the hardways, bet the hard ten, the point, make it come out, bring it out with a hardway bet."

These are just some examples of the patter stickmen use. Most of the time, though, the stickman is after the players to make hardway bets, for often these bets are made for the dealers by the players, who might announce "one and one" when giving their chips to the stickman. By this term, the player is instructing the stickman to bet one chip for the player and one for "the boys," the common term used for the dealers when betting for them.

Some stickmen are very good at making a table hum, and players like a lively table. A good stickman can also help the casino, for if he makes the game exciting, the players react enthusiastically by making more frequent and larger bets.

The Dealers "On Base"

At the craps table the person you deal directly with is one of the two standing dealers, on base, who stand on either side of the seated boxman. Each dealer covers one end of the identical sections of the craps layout.

Let's assume you have a couple of hundred dollars, ready for action. If you want casino chips, you catch the attention of the dealer on your side of the table and put your cash down on the layout. The dealer picks up the money and hands it to the boxman to be counted.

The boxman counts the cash and verifies the amount

with you. Next, the boxman authorizes the dealer to give you casino chips in that amount, and puts the cash into a slot on the table in front of him, and "socks" the money into a dropbox, which is concealed under the table.

The game can be played with currency, but casinos prefer that you play with their chips. All payoffs are made in chips, even if you bet cash. The denominations of the chips are usually $1, $5, $100, and $500.

In addition to giving you casino chips for your cash, the dealer will also "change color," that is, change your chips into either larger or smaller denominations at your convenience during play. All you have to do is give your chips to the dealer and say "change color." You can refer to $5 chips as "nickels," $25 chips as "quarters," and $100 chips as "dollars."

When you win your bets, you are paid off by the standing dealer. If you lose your bets, the dealer removes your chips from the layout and either keeps them in front of him or gives them to the boxman.

Although you'll be able to make a great many bets by yourself on the layout, such as pass line, come, field, and don't come, for example, there are some bets only the dealer can place for you and handle properly. For example, the dealer makes all place bets and takes all odds bets on come and don't come. After a come number is established, the dealer removes your chips from the betting area and places them in the correct number box. If you want to make a center or proposition bet, give your chips to the dealer to pass them to the stickman, who controls and handles all center wagers.

Each standing dealer has a marker puck, or plastic disk, in front of him. Before a come-out roll, the puck is lying on its black side, labeled "Off," in the don't-come box. Once a point has been established by the shooter, the puck is turned on its white side, labeled "On," and moved by the dealer to the place-number box corresponding to the point.

As you come to the table to make a bet, always look for the marker puck. If it's lying on the white side in a place-number box, you cannot make any line bet because a point has already been established.

If players have any questions about any aspect of the game they should direct them to the standing dealer. The dealer is there not only to help the players with their bets, but to give them service, and this includes information about the game that the bettor might not know.

For instance, if a player wants to know the maximum free odds permitted on a line bet, or wants to know if double free odds are allowed, he or she should ask the dealer. Or a player might want to know the minimum and maximum limits at the table before putting his chips on the layout. If the dealer is competent and shows an interest in the player's action, not only will the game be more enjoyable for the bettor, but the casino will prosper as well.

THE BOXMAN

The boxman is a casino executive who is in charge of the craps table while he's sitting at it between the two standing dealers. Generally, one boxman is assigned to each craps table, but when the action is fast and furious and high rollers are playing at crowded tables, there may be two boxmen sitting side by side.

The boxman's main duty is to supervise both the casino bankroll and the craps game, which are linked together. If improper payouts are made, then the casino bankroll is going to suffer. Or if there is collusion between the dealers and players, the bankroll is also going to be dented. So, the boxman watches the game closely to make certain that it is run properly and that the chips changing hands are correct.

The major portion of the casino bankroll on the table is under the supervision of the boxman. The stacks of chips are directly in front of him, and, if necessary, he can wrap his arms around the stacks. It is his duty to protect that bankroll.

If one boxman is on duty, he watches one side of the table, supervising the dealer at that end, and it is the duty of the stickman to watch the other end of the table. When two boxmen are on duty, each watches over one side of the table.

If the dice are thrown off the table by a shooter, they must first be examined by the boxman before they're returned to the game. He twirls each die around to look for the casino logo, the coded number, and any changes in the surface of the die to make certain that it has not been tampered with.

When a dispute occurs at the table between a player and a dealer, as sometimes happens, the boxman has the final say in settling the argument. In some casinos, the player is given the benefit of the doubt the first time, but thereafter, he will be ruled against if the same dispute comes up.

THE PIT AND ITS PERSONNEL

Craps tables are arranged in a casino with a particular purpose in mind. Several tables form what is known as a "pit," an oval-shape arrangement of craps tables, set up so that the standing dealers and boxmen have their backs to the interior of the pit, whereas the stickman stands with his back to the aisle where customers and people go by freely. Players are not allowed into the pit. This arrangement is worked out so that other executive employees of the casino can stand directly behind the dealers and boxmen and watch them closely. The dealers are watched the most carefully because they are constantly handling the casino chips in their collection and payoffs.

The men and women in the pit, known as "floormen," are considered casino executives, except for the pit bookkeeper.

Floormen

Floormen stand in the pit and watch the play at a particular table or group of tables, depending upon the action. They pick up on whatever might be missed by the boxman and the stickman after the dice are rolled and, because they are standing, they often get a better view of the activity at the table than the boxman.

Floormen wear suits or sports jackets, not the uniforms of the casino, because they are executives. Their main duty, besides watching the game itself, is to deal with players who want credit at the tables.

When players request chips on credit, the floorman asks their names, then verifies their credit line at the casino. The floorman can do this in a number of ways, but with the automated and computerized features prevalent in modern casinos, players' names can be run on a computer scan right in the pit. In casinos that don't have this feature, the floorman has the pit bookkeeper call the cashier's cage to verify the players' credit line.

If the credit is approved, the floorman authorizes the dealer to give the players chips to bet with, and then, a couple of minutes later, the floorman brings a slip of paper to each player and has the player sign a marker, or IOU, for that amount of chips.

When a player has finished betting and is about to leave the table, if a winner, the boxman or floorman will insist that the marker be paid off then and there. If a loser, the player is allowed to cash in the remaining chips at the cashier's cage, and the marker stands against the player's overall credit.

In some casinos, the floorman sits on a high chair or "ladder" overlooking the game. This has become an archaic method of supervision, although it is used sometimes in casinos such as the Four Queens in downtown Las Vegas. Here, the floorman is known as the "ladderman."

The Pit Boss

Controlling the entire craps pit is the pit boss, who is rarely seen by the players and seldom comes into contact with them. Most players mistakenly refer to floormen as pit bosses. Floormen work directly under a pit boss and don't have the power that he has.

The pit boss is responsible for all the craps tables making up the pit. What he is basically concerned with is profits. If the pit is profitable, the pit boss's work is easy. But should a table get "hot" and the players take away a great deal of money, making the pit shift unprofitable, then the pit boss goes on the carpet to his bosses to explain away the losses.

Some pit bosses and other supervisory personnel, whose main interest is a profitable shift, become quite superstitious when things are not going their way. They may ask the shooter to change the way he throws the dice, or watch the shooter closely ("sweating the action"), or they might, in extreme cases, send in a whole new crew of dealers.

TIPPING, OR TOKING, THE DEALERS

In craps, the crew of four dealers share all tips or "tokes," a casino term for tips, given to them during the course of their workshift. These tokes are not shared with any other casino personnel. Because dealers work for small salaries, ranging from $25 to $35 a day, they depend on tips for the better part of their income. They are usually tipped for friendly, courteous, and efficient service to players.

Most bettors bet hardways or other center, or proposition, wagers for the dealers, bets which pay off in multiples, so that a $1 bet on a hard 6, paying at odds of 10 for 1, for example, will net the dealers $10. After a bet has won, the dealers must remove the wager from the table because usually they are not allowed to parlay their wins.

Dealers know that the center proposition bets are poor ones, with prohibitive odds. They prefer line or come bets to be made for them, with a better chance of winning. Some players, instead of betting for the boys, simply tip dealers directly with casino chips during or after play.

What should you tip a dealer? First of all, remember that a toke or winning bet made for them is shared by just that crew on shift. If you have been given good service by a dealer, or if the dealer is friendly and efficient, then he or she should be tipped something for the good work. The amount of the tip depends on several factors: the two most important are the size of your bets and the amount you've won or lost.

Obviously, if you are a small bettor, you are not expected to toke the dealers heavily. If you are a big winner, you probably tip better than if you are losing a lot of money.

If you're betting $25 chips and getting good service from a dealer, an occasional $5 bet for the boys on the come or on the line will be appreciated. If you're betting $5 chips, an occasional $1 bet will also be appreciated.

If you've been losing heavily, the dealers understand your reluctance to give away more chips with big tokes, but if you've been treated well by the dealers, you can still make an occasional bet for them.

Remember, you're not forced to bet for the dealers or to toke them, but common courtesy should be used. These men and women are doing a tough job, and if they've been friendly and helpful, they should be rewarded.

Sometimes a dealer's alertness can save or make you a lot of money. If you forget to remove a winning bet, the dealer will point this out to you. Should you forget to back up a line or come bet with proper free odds, an efficient dealer will also point this out. Dealers who take an interest in the players can show them the maximum odds bets permitted, which may turn out to be quite profitable for the bettors.

13

If a dealer is unfriendly or hostile, or constantly pushes for tokes, I would not recommend tipping at all. Dealers can really make a player feel uncomfortable if they have the wrong attitude. Casino executives watch not only the action but the way the dealers treat the bettors.

If a crew of dealers is pushing for chips to be bet for them, or is handling the bettors badly, that crew may be chastised and, in extreme cases, fired from their jobs. The casino's profits often depend upon public relations, and it is the crew of dealers that the public most often deals with directly at the craps table.

II

THE DICE: THE COMBINATIONS AND TRUE ODDS

THE DICE

The game of casino craps is basically a dice game in which the numbers that come up after they are thrown determine the outcome of the players' bets.

Two dice are used in the craps shoot, each die a nearly perfect cube having six sides. Each side is imprinted with from one to six dots, representing the numbers 1 to 6.

Practically all of us have played games with dice at one time or another, games such as Monopoly and backgammon. But the dice used in casino craps are not quite the same as games dice, although they produce the same combinations when rolled.

First, most games dice are not transparent, but all casino craps dice are. If you hold a casino die to the light, you can see right through to the opposite side and count the dots there. Transparency serves a purpose, because when dice can be looked through, any weighting device inserted by a cheat can easily be seen. And the casinos want to make certain that the games they run are honest and aboveboard, for any cheating that goes on can only hurt the casinos.

Second, the dice are larger than ordinary games dice,

approximately ¾″ square on each side. These dice are manufactured to exacting standards, so that each die is almost a perfect cube, and only measurements in the thousandths of an inch reveal any deviation from perfection.

Casino dice are made so that their corners are ultrasharp. If they are rolled on wood, for example, they would quickly destroy the finish of the wood by perforating and nicking the grain. Dice are destructive instruments when thrown forcefully, and casinos must continually replace the felt surfaces of the tables the dice land on.

As mentioned before, the casinos want to run an honest game, for a dishonest game can only hurt them. Casinos make an enormous profit from craps games. Several years ago an independent study revealed that the average craps table on the Las Vegas Strip yielded a profit of close to one million dollars a year. Therefore, casinos are satisfied to make their money the easy and honest way. When cheating occurs, it is usually against the casino, but innocent players also get burned by crooked dice. If security were lax, then cheats would zero in on certain casinos, and once word got around that the game was suspect, the high rollers and other honest players would stay away.

To protect themselves, casinos buy the best and most carefully manufactured dice, and imprint both the casino logo and coded numbers on each die. These dice, usually about six or eight in number, are introduced into a game during one workshift; their coded numbers are recorded by a casino executive. After the shift is over, the dice are replaced by other coded dice, so that a cheat cannot manufacture his own dice with a standard coded number.

During the course of a game, if a single die or both dice are accidentally thrown off the table, the die or dice must be examined by the boxman before being put back into play. He checks the numbers, and looks for any imperfections such as nicks and cuts in the dice.

All of these precautions are necessary since craps is a

game that involves a lot of money, and a cheat who introduces crooked dice can quickly make a small fortune unless the casino employees are alert.

During the course of a long series of rolls by one shooter, the dice are constantly turned over by the stickman, to make certain that each die has from one to six dots on its sides. If a player examines a single die he would notice one dot on one side and six dots on the opposite side, and any two opposing sides of the die will total 7. If crooked dice containing only even numbers were introduced, a 7 could never come up, and cheats could ruin the casino bankroll in a short period of time.

THE COMBINATIONS

Two dice, each having six sides, are used in casino craps. They can be thrown together in thirty-six possible combinations. Table 1 shows these combinations.

TABLE 1

Number	Combinations	Ways to Roll
2	1–1	1
3	1–2, 2–1	2
4	1–3, 3–1, 2–2	3
5	1–4, 4–1, 2–3, 3–2	4
6	1–5, 5–1, 2–4, 4–2, 3–3	5
7	1–6, 6–1, 2–5, 5–2, 3–4, 4–3	6
8	2–6, 6–2, 3–5, 5–3, 4–4	5
9	3–6, 6–3, 4–5, 5–4	4
10	4–6, 6–4, 5–5	3
11	5–6, 6–5	2
12	6–6	1

There is a definite symmetry to the above table, with the 7 standing in the center. The 7 is unique in that it can be made no matter what number shows on one die, and it can be made in the most ways—six. The 7 is the most important number in craps, for it determines many of the collections and payoffs.

TRUE ODDS

The Point Numbers

The point numbers in the game of craps are 4, 5, 6, 8, 9, and 10. Table 1 shows that none of these numbers can be made in as many ways as 7 can, and, therefore, the odds against any of them repeating before a 7 shows on the dice is better than even money. Table 2 shows these odds.

TABLE 2

Number	Ways to Roll	True Odds Against Repeating Before a 7 Is Rolled
4	3	2 to 1
5	4	3 to 2
6	5	6 to 5
8	5	6 to 5
9	4	3 to 2
10	3	2 to 1

One-Roll Wagers

Certain one-roll bets are allowed in casino craps, where the player bets that a certain number will show on the very next throw of the dice. Table 3 shows these numbers and the true odds against their appearing. To figure out these odds, we must remember that there are thirty-six possible combinations on the dice.

18

TABLE 3

Number	Ways to Roll	True Odds Against Repeating on Next Roll
2	1	35 to 1
3	2	17 to 1
7	6	5 to 1
11	2	17 to 1
12	1	35 to 1

These are some of the odds you will encounter as you play casino craps, and the other combinations and odds important to you will be discussed fully in subsequent sections of this book.

III

THE CRAPS TABLE AND LAYOUT

THE TABLE

Casino craps is played on a felt-covered area the size of a large billiards table. Around that area are walls forming the table itself, against which the players stand and on which are rails holding their chips. There is no one standard for the tables used by the casinos, so their sizes depend on how many players a particular club wishes to accommodate at its tables. This number generally runs from twelve to twenty-four participants.

Most players do not like the very large tables because of the length, which makes it difficult to see the dice thrown to the far end. A more comfortable arrangement seems to be a table holding from eighteen to twenty bettors. The table is divided so that half the players are at one end and half at the other, with casino personnel in between the two groups. Each player's spot is partitioned off by dividing lines on a grooved rail running along the area where the bettors stand.

The dividing line for each player is rather narrow, and a table accommodating twenty players would create a tight fit if all the spaces were taken up by the players. After all, players move around, waving their arms and twisting their bodies as the action on the table gets them involved. For all players to be really comfortable, at least one space on each end must be forfeited. Thus, a table holding twenty players could really accommodate eighteen easily.

But when the action is hot and heavy, or when the casino is packed, the players somehow wedge themselves into place to get into the game. They stand sideways, they suck in their stomachs, they try not to move, in order to be able to play. Even the dealers get uncomfortable at these crowded tables, especially the stickman, who stands in the middle of the outside of the table, and bettors may crowd in on him.

THE LAYOUT

What all players want at a craps table is to bet on the game; they want to get in on the action. The area that is involved with their wagers, which shows all the possible bets, is called the "layout." The layout is the printed felt material of the craps table, which divides the table into various segments and betting areas and shows the different types of wagers by name, along with some of the odds paid on these bets.

The following is a craps layout, the standard imprint found at many tables. There may be slight differences from city to city or jurisdiction to jurisdiction, and even from casino to casino, but the bets shown, and the ones we'll be explaining, are the ones you will find when you're at the craps table.

The standard color of the felt is green, with the dividing lines either white or yellow. Sometimes the surface is of a different color, to match the décor of a particular casino, and the layout may be printed in various colors to satisfy the taste of some interior decorator or designer.

The layout shown is the one found in the northern Nevada and Atlantic City casinos, as well as in most of the

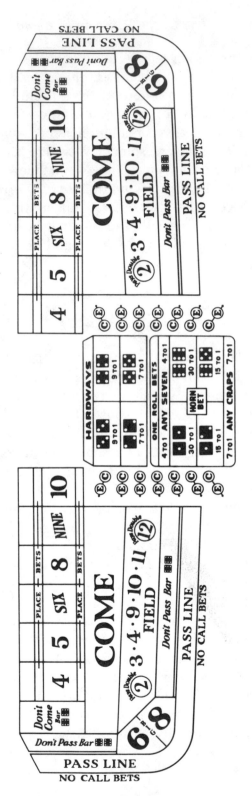

Nevada layout
Las Vegas, Nevada

downtown Las Vegas clubs. There may be minor differences as to the various casinos, and the Las Vegas Strip casino layouts are usually slightly different as well. Once you understand the bets on the illustrated layout, however, you'll be able to play anywhere in America with confidence.

Some foreign casinos, not under the control of gaming commissions, may alter their layout, omitting or adding certain bets. The British casinos may make the payoffs on certain wagers more favorable to the player than the American casinos. In addition, the British often change the name of Pass and Don't Pass to Win and Don't Win, terms more easily understood by laymen and novices.

On the layout we notice first of all that there are three distinct areas. The two side sections are identical to each other, whereas in the center there is a maze of bets unlike those in the other two areas.

The center of the layout is the home of the center, or proposition, bets, not one of which is worthwhile. In other words, if a bettor did not wager on the center bets, he'd be much better off in the long run. This part of the layout is under the control of the stickman, who places and calls out winning and losing bets as they occur.

The two end sections have betting areas both favorable and unfavorable to the bettor. Each area is serviced by a standing dealer, who deals directly with the players in the course of the game, collecting losing wagers, paying off winning bets, and sometimes handling the bets for the players in certain betting situations.

Later we're going to discuss all the bets found on the layout and the important free-odds bet not advertised on the layout, one at a time, in full, and whether or not they are favorable to the players. If certain bets should be made, we'll explain why, and also explain why other bets should be avoided.

Before we go into the various bets allowed on the layout, we'll cover the basic game in the next chapter, so that you'll know how the game is played, won, or lost.

IV

THE BASIC GAME

The game of casino craps evolved from the street games and private games of craps played for hundreds of years in America, and for thousands of years in various forms in many different cultures around the world.

Casino craps is a much more involved and elaborate game than the street game, for in the street game players bet against one another and there are no dealers or other personnel to help out with the bets. The game is simpler in order to allow players to know just what is going on at every moment. The casino game, however, doesn't have to be that elementary. The dealers handle many of the bets, and bets not handled by the dealers are placed in clearly marked betting areas by the players.

Still, the heart of the casino game is the basic game played for many years on the streets, in private apartments, and wherever gambling men and women get together with a pair of dice.

THE SHOOTER

One person at a time holds the dice and throws them, and this player is called the "shooter." While the shooter is rolling the dice, all the other bettors at the game are affected by the throws. When they bet on the basic game, they are betting either with or against the dice, and it is what the shooter rolls that determines whether they win or lose their individual wagers.

The shooter at casino craps is selected arbitrarily. One or two players may be at the table when a game is opened up by the house, and the stickman will ask one of them to shoot the dice.

After the first shooter has been selected, the dice move around the table in a clockwise direction, from right to left, and each player at the table has the opportunity to become the shooter. Any player may refuse the dice and forfeit his or her turn to be the shooter. There is no obligation to roll them, nor, on the other hand, is there any stigma involved when refusing the dice.

The shooter is usually given between six and eight dice from which he or she selects two. The shooter may later decide to change the dice, although this is rarely done, but it is the shooter's privilege. In some of the illegal private clubs in America, after each roll, the dice are changed so that no marked or crooked dice can be thrown for more than one roll at a time. In the legitimate casinos, however, where the dice are carefully scrutinized and marked with both the casino's logo and coded numbers, once the shooter selects two dice, he can roll them as long as he wants to. No dealer or other casino employee can take them away, unless they have been found to be tampered with or damaged in the course of a roll. The dice may be examined by the boxman and the stickman, but the dice remain in play as long as the shooter cares to have them.

In the casino game, after the shooter selects the dice, he or she is required to make a line bet, either pass or don't pass, before the roll. Practically all shooters bet on the pass line with the dice, although some shooters bet against their own roll. The house doesn't care which bet they make as long as it's a line bet.

The shooter is supposed to throw the dice with enough force to hit the farthest wall of the table. If the shooter misses the wall or the throw is so weak that the dice don't reach the wall, on the next roll the shooter will be told to throw them harder.

If the shooter continually misses the wall, the dice may be taken away, or the roll declared void by the boxman. The casino employees are always concerned with cheats, and they believe that a random bounce is achieved if both dice hit the far wall. Some cheats can control the dice in such a manner that if no barrier is struck they can literally "run the scales" from 2 to 12 on the dice. Cheating is all the casino cares about, and no matter how eccentric your roll, you won't be bothered as long as you bounce those dice off the opposite wall of the table.

THE COME-OUT ROLL

The come-out roll is the most important roll in the game of casino craps. A come-out roll occurs whenever a point has not yet been established. This can occur under the following conditions:

• A new shooter is given the dice and has not yet made the first throw. The shooter is said to be "coming out" and the first roll is a "come-out" roll.

• When a shooter has rolled a 7 before repeating the established point number. The shooter is said to have "sevened-out," and his or her shoot is at an end. The next roll of the dice by a new shooter is a come-out roll.

• A shooter has rolled a 7 or 11 on the first throw of the dice, or on a previous come-out roll. A 7 or 11 is a winner on the pass line, and the shooter now has a new come-out roll.

• When a shooter, on the initial or come-out roll, throws a 2, 3, or 12. These rolls are immediate losers for the pass-line bettor, and the shooter is said to have "crapped out." After this throw, a new come-out roll occurs.

• When a shooter has rolled a point number in the previous come-out roll and repeats the number before rolling a 7. This is a win for a pass-line bettor, and after the point has repeated, there is a new come-out roll.

THE LINE BETS: PASS LINE AND DON'T PASS

The line bets are the basic wagers of casino craps. Many other bets may be made on the layout and often are, but the line bets constitute the heart of the game, and the winning and losing of these wagers often determine the results of other bets made by players on the layout.

A line bet can be made only before the come-out roll, and sometimes this bet may be won or lost on the come out. However, many times the result of the line bet isn't decided until the dice have been thrown a number of times.

Practically all players at the table make some kind of line bet, either pass line—betting right—or don't pass—betting wrong. About 90 percent of the bettors at the table bet with the dice on the pass line, for reasons explained later.

The Pass Line

The pass-line betting area runs almost the full length of the players' standing area, in order for each player to make this bet easily. It is the most popular bet on the layout, and is made by the majority of players.

The bet can be made only before the come-out roll by placing the chip or chips in the area marked "pass line." The pass line is also known as the "front line."

A player betting pass line is known as a "right bettor." A player betting against the dice on don't pass is called a "wrong bettor," but there is no moral connotation attached to either of these terms. They are simply common designations used for many years at casino craps tables for these types of bettors.

A pass-line, or right, bettor wins under the following circumstances:

• The shooter on the come-out roll throws a 7 or 11. These two numbers are known as "naturals" and the player betting pass line is paid off immediately at even money.

• The shooter on the come-out roll throws a 4, 5, 6, 8, 9, or 10 (known as point numbers) and repeats the point number before rolling a 7. When this is accomplished, the shooter is said to have "made his point," and the pass-line bettor wins, also at even money.

Suppose the shooter rolled a 6 on the come-out roll. The dealers move the marker pucks to the place-number box 6 to indicate that 6 is the point. For the pass-line bettors to win their wagers, the shooter must repeat the number 6, the point, before rolling a 7. All other numbers become immaterial to pass-line bets.

Let's assume that after rolling the initial 6, the shooter threw the following numbers: 4, 11, 5, 5, 8, and 6. The pass-line bettors win their wagers because the 6 was repeated before a 7 came up on the dice.

All the other numbers, including the 11, wouldn't count, even though the 11 would have been a winner on the come-out roll. Also, the repeating 5s wouldn't count either, because the point was 6, not 5. It is the come-out roll that determines the point for pass-line bettors, and once that point is established, only that number and the 7 concern the right bettors.

The following are losing rolls for pass-line bettors.

• The shooter on the come-out roll throws a 2, 3, or 12, all known as "craps." The shooter is said to have "crapped out" and all pass-line bets go down the drain with these rolls, but the dice are still retained by the shooter.

• The shooter, having established a point (4, 5, 6, 8, 9, or

10) on the come-out roll, rolls a 7 before repeating the point.

To make this concept clearer, let's assume that the come-out roll was a 9, which is now the point. The shooter has to repeat this number for the pass-line bettors to win. The following numbers were thrown after the 9 was established: 6, 8, 4, 2, 12, 11, 6, and 7. When the 7 was rolled, the shooter "sevened-out," or lost, for all pass-line bettors because the 7 came up before the 9 was repeated.

For purposes of this roll, it did not matter that 6 repeated twice, because 9 was the point, not 6, and all other numbers rolled during the course of the shoot were likewise immaterial to pass-line bettors.

The following sequence of rolls are losing ones for pass-line bettors:

- 8 (point), 6, 9, 10, 10, 7.
- 10 (point), 8, 4, 4, 6, 7.

In both cases 7 came up on the dice before the point number was repeated, and thus the shooter sevened-out. After a seven out, the shooter loses not only the pass-line bet, but the dice as well to the next shooter. A shooter can hold the dice only until a seven out.

To summarize the pass-line bet. It wins if:

- A 7 or 11 is thrown on the come-out roll.
- A point number is rolled on the come out and repeats before a 7 is thrown.

It loses if:

- A 2, 3, or 12 is rolled on the come-out roll.
- A point number is made on the come-out roll, but a 7 comes up on the dice before the point is repeated.

A pass-line bet, once made by a player, cannot be removed or reduced.

Don't Pass

The don't-pass betting area is much smaller than the pass-line betting space, since far fewer players bet against the dice.

Don't-pass bettors are known also as wrong bettors, and this wager is known as a "back-line" bet. It is almost but not quite diametrically opposite to the pass-line wager.

A don't-pass bet, like the pass-line bet, can be made only prior to the come-out roll. It is done by putting the chip or chips on the don't-pass box. Once the bet is made, the don't-pass bettor wins in the following ways:

• The shooter rolls a 2 or 3 on the come-out roll. This is an immediate winner for the don't-pass bettor, who gets paid off at even money.

Note that we left out the 12. The 12 is barred as a winner on the don't pass, and the bet becomes a standoff, neither winning nor losing, even though it is a loser for the pass-line bettor. The house bars the 12 to preserve its advantage of 1.4 percent over the don't-pass bettor. If the 12 is a winner for the wrong bettor, then the don't-pass bettor would have an edge over the house on this bet.

In some casinos, such as the ones in northern Nevada, the 2 instead of the 12 is barred to the don't-pass bettors. It is immaterial which number is barred, the 2 or 12, since either number can be made only by one combination of the dice. When the 2 is barred, then the 3 and 12 are immediate winners for the don't-pass bettors.

• The shooter rolls a point number (4, 5, 6, 8, 9, or 10) on the come out, and then rolls a 7 before repeating the point. This is a win for the don't-pass bettor at even money.

The following examples of sequences are winning ones for the don't-pass bettor:

• 6 (point), 5, 8, 9, 10, 12, 2, 4, 7
• 5 (point), 9, 8, 8, 9, 11, 7

A wrong or don't-pass bettor loses the wager under the following conditions:

• If a shooter rolls a 7 or 11 on the come-out roll. This is an immediate loser for don't-pass bettors.

• If a shooter rolls a point number on the come out and repeats it before throwing a 7.

The following examples of sequences are losing ones for the don't-pass bettors because the point was repeated before a 7 was thrown:

• 4 (point), 5, 12, 3, 2, 8, 4.
• 8 (point), 9, 11, 2, 4, 5, 10, 8.

To summarize the don't-pass bet:

• The don't-pass bettor wins immediately and is paid off at even money if a 2 or 3 is rolled on the come out.

• If a 12 is rolled on the come out, the bet is a standoff. In some casinos the 2 is barred instead and the bet is a standoff if the 2 is thrown on the come out. In that case, the 3 and 12 are immediate winners for the don't-pass bettor.

• If a 7 or 11 is rolled on the come out it is an immediate loser for the don't-pass bettor.

• Should a point number be rolled on the come out and a 7 is thrown before the point is repeated, the don't-pass bettor wins the wager at even money.

• Should a point number be rolled on the come out and that number repeats before a 7 is thrown by the shooter, the don't-pass bettor loses.

Once a don't-pass bet is made it can always be removed by the player after the point number is established, since the odds favor the don't-pass bettor over the house. If the point is 6 or 8, the wrong bettor has an advantage of 6 to 5; if it's 5 or 9, the advantage increases to 3 to 2; and the point 4 or 10 gives the wrong bettor an advantage of 2 to 1 on the bet.

The odds are in favor of the don't-pass bettor after the

31

point is established because 7 can be made in six different ways, while the other point numbers cannot be made in more than 5 ways on 6 or 8, four ways on 5 or 9, and three ways on the 4 or 10.

Although the casino allows the don't-pass bettor to remove the wager after a point has been established on the come-out roll, it should never be done, because the odds favor the wrong bettor at this time.

Although there are relatively fewer don't-pass than pass-line bettors, the difference in the odds is negligible. The pass-line, or right, bettor wagering on the pass line gives the house a 1.41 percent advantage, while the don't-pass, or wrong, bettor gives away 1.4 percent to the casino.

V

THE FREE-ODDS BETS

The free-odds bet is the most important bet a player can make at the casino craps table. But if you examine the entire layout, you won't find this wager listed. Therefore, many players, even those with experience, do not make free-odds wagers, and thus they deprive themselves of the opportunity to maximize their profits at the craps table.

Why the bet is not shown on the layout is not clear, for it is a wager made by all astute players and is an integral part of the game of craps, whether played on the street or in the casino. However, rather than chastise the gaming commissions, we'll explain the bet fully so that you can use it to best advantage.

A free-odds bet may be made by any line bettor as well as by players betting come and don't come. It is the only bet in the game of casino craps where the house has no advantage or edge over the player. That's why it's called a "free-odds" bet. Every other bet gives the house some type of edge over the player, no matter how small, but the free-odds bet puts the player even with the casino. If only free-odds bets were allowed at a craps table, the casino would never make a penny's profit on the game. Perhaps that's one reason casinos don't show the bet.

FREE ODDS: THE PASS LINE

After making the pass-line bet and a point has been established, the player can make a free-odds bet in an amount less than, equal to, or, in some instances, greater than the pass-line bet. This additional wager is made by placing chips behind the pass line, directly behind the chips bet on the pass line.

When this free-odds bet is made, the house pays the winner the correct odds against the number repeating before the 7 shows on the dice. The odds against all of the point numbers are repeated here:

Number	*Odds Against*
4 or 10	2 to 1
5 or 9	3 to 2
6 or 8	6 to 5

It is these odds, either 6 to 5, 3 to 2, or 2 to 1, that the casino pays on the free-odds bet, depending on the point number. Let's assume that you've bet $10 on the pass line and the come-out roll is 4. You are permitted to bet an additional $10 behind the pass line, behind the original $10 bet, as a free-odds bet. If you win, you are paid $10, or even money, on the pass-line wager, and $20, or 2 to 1, on the free-odds bet for a total win of $30. Of course, if you lose your bets, you'll lose $20, including both the pass-line and free-odds bets.

Table 1 shows the payoffs on a $10 free-odds bet, depending on the point number thrown on the come-out roll.

TABLE 1

Number	*Free-Odds Bet*	*Odds*	*Payoff*
4 or 10	$10	2 to 1	$20
5 or 9	$10	3 to 2	$15
6 or 8	$10	6 to 5	$12

These payoffs are in addition to the pass-line win of $10 at even money. Thus, if 4 or 10 was the point and won, the total payoff would be $30; if 5 or 9 won, the payoff would be $25; and if 6 or 8 was the point and won, the total payoff would be $22. If any of these bets lost, the total loss would be the same no matter what the point was, and that is $20.

When the house permits an amount equal to the line bet to be wagered as a free-odds bet, it is permitting *single odds* to be taken by the pass-line bettor. When the casino allows double the line bet to be made as a free-odds bet, it is permitting *double odds* to be taken.

Most casinos, including many in Las Vegas and Lake Tahoe as well as all those in Atlantic city, permit only single odds to be taken by the pass-line bettor. When single odds are allowed, the house edge drops from 1.41 percent down to 0.8 percent on the combined line and free-odds bets.

When double odds are allowed, the house edge drops even further, down to 0.6 percent. Thus, double odds, if permitted, should always be made, not only because the house advantage is lower, but also because the player stands to make much more money should numbers repeat and points be made.

Even in casinos that allow only single-odds bets, the dealers allow you to make more than single-odds wagers equal to the pass-line bet, and these wagers should be learned and taken advantage of. These situations come up when the bet is an unequal amount, such as $5 or $25 on the pass line and the point is either 5 or 9. Since the correct payoff is 3 to 2 on free-odds bets, a $5 bet would have to be paid off at $7.50, and a $25 bet at $37.50. Since few casinos use half-dollars at their craps tables, the payoff would be reduced to $7 and $37 respectively, which is slightly less than 3 to 2.

Therefore, in this situation, the casino permits you to bet $6 behind the line as a free-odds bet after you've bet $5 on the pass line, if the point is 5 or 9. The payoff is then $9 for $6 if you win your bet. With a $25 wager on the pass line and the same point established, the casino permits you to bet $30 as a free-odds bet, to be paid off at $45 for $30 if you win your bet. This works for all unequal amounts bet on the pass line when the point is 5 or 9. A $15 pass-line bet allows you to bet $20 behind the line, and a $35 pass-line bet allows you to bet $40 behind the line as a free-odds bet.

The other situation in which you are permitted a larger free-odds bet even when only single odds are permitted involves 6 or 8 as the point. If you have bet *three units* on the pass line and the point is either 6 or 8, the house permits you to bet *five units* behind the line as a free-odds bet. We're talking about *units* now instead of sums, because it doesn't matter if you bet $3, $15, or even $75 or $300, the same rule applies. In all these cases, you are permitted to bet, respectively, $5, $25, $125, and $500 as free-odds bets.

Other bets on the pass line also can be worked out with the same formula. If you bet $60 on the pass line and the point is either 6 or 8, you can bet $100 as a free-odds wager, because you've bet three units of $20 each, and can now back them up with five units of $20 each, or $100. If in doubt about how much you can bet as a free-odds wager if the point is 6 or 8, ask the dealer, who will tell you the maximum bet allowed behind the line. We always suggest wagering three units as a pass-line bet in any single-odds house because 6 and 8 come up as point numbers more frequently than any other points, and you'll be able to take advantage of maximum free odds when 6 or 8 is the point.

By making use of these two situations, you'll not only have a chance to win more money, but will drive the house advantage down to the very bottom limit in a single-odds casino.

A point number of 4 or 10 pays off at 2 to 1 on the free-odds bets, so there's never any difficulty in making these free-odds wagers in the correct amount. The casino allows you to bet only an amount equal to the pass-line bet as a free-odds wager when 4 or 10 is the point.

Since the house has no advantage on the free-odds bets,

and since they lower the overall house advantage over the player, the casino permits free-odds bets to be removed or reduced at any time by the player, but the player should never do this.

Double Odds

Some casinos in downtown Las Vegas and on the Vegas Strip allow you to bet double the amount of your pass-line wager as a free-odds bet. The rules of the Las Vegas casinos change from time to time, so we are not able to give you a complete list of casinos permitting double odds.

Casinos that do allow double odds often advertise this fact on the marquees, but if you have any doubts, ask the dealer at the table. If you want to play craps and are unsure of the rules of the particular casino, always ask about double odds, for it is to your advantage to play at a table that allows them.

In Lake Tahoe, most of the casinos permit only single odds, but Reno clubs as a rule allow double odds at practically every craps table in town. In Atlantic City, only single odds are permitted in all the casinos established as of this writing. If you're playing craps in Atlantic City, you won't find a double-odds craps game, but follow our advice and make three-unit wagers at a single-odds game so that you can take advantage of the enhanced odds allowed if the point is 5, 6, 8, or 9.

When double odds are allowed, the casino permits you to wager *double* your pass-line bet as a free-odds bet. If you bet $10 on the line, you can bet $20 behind the line as a free-odds wager, no matter what the point is.

There is one slight exception to this rule—in favor of the player. Casinos allow you to bet *five units* as a free-odds bet even if you had bet *two units* on the pass line and the point is either 6 or 8.

Let's assume that you've bet $10 on the pass line. This works out to two units of $5 chips. The point is 8. Now, you can wager $25, or five units of $5 chips, behind the pass line. This rule is definitely to your advantage, so take care to make the maximum wager permitted by the casino when the point is 6 or 8.

When double odds are allowed, the house edge is reduced to 0.6 percent, and is the lowest edge the casino has over the player, except for the free-odds bet, which is paid off at correct odds.

Double-odds bets, like all free-odds wagers, can always be reduced or removed by the players, but this should never be done, for it is to the advantage of the player to have as much money out on the odds bets as possible when betting right. The payoffs can really add up.

For example, if you bet $25 on the pass line and the point is 4, and then put $50 behind the line, should the point be made, you would win a total of $125. If you lost your bets, you would lose only $75. With double odds and a hot roll going, you can make a lot of money at the craps table.

There have been several cases of $200,000 or larger wins at double-odds games in Las Vegas, when players at the table took advantage of maximum free odds and had a hot shoot going with many points made and numbers repeating. I know two casinos that discontinued double odds because they were afraid of repeating astronomical losses. If the casinos are afraid of the double-odds games, then that's the best reason I can give you to seek out double-odds tables when playing craps.

If you're a right bettor at craps in Las Vegas, play at a double-odds game. Look for the casino that features these odds, and play there; it will definitely be to your benefit.

FREE ODDS: COME BETS

Come bets will be fully explained in a later section, but you should know that you can also make free-odds bets on your come wagers. Briefly, a come bet is the same as a pass-line wager, except that a come bet can be made only after a point is established.

After you've made a come bet and a come number—which is 4, 5, 6, 8, 9, or 10, the same as point numbers—is established, you make free-odds wager by giving your chips to the dealer to place on your come bets, which have been taken by the dealer and placed in the appropriate place-number box. All you have to do is tell the dealer, "Odds on the come," and your chips will be placed on top of the come bet at a slight offset, to differentiate the two types of wagers.

If you win your bet, you'll be paid off just as if you had made a pass-line wager. Where single odds are allowed, the rules applying to single odds work, including the enhanced free-odds bets on the 5, 6, 8, and 9. Where double odds are permitted, you are allowed to make a five-unit odds bet on 6 or 8 as a come number if your original come bet was only two units.

Free-odds bets can always be removed or reduced by the player, but we recommend you never do this on your come or other bets.

FREE ODDS: DON'T PASS

The wrong bettor can also make free-odds bets, but this player is *laying* odds, not taking them, and thus is putting out more money than what will be won on the free-odds wager. This is not to say the wrong bettor loses money on the winning bet. If $10 is laid as a free-odds bet against the 4, for example, the player gets back only $5 plus the original $10 bet. By laying the odds, the wrong bettor is getting back 1 for 2. If the player was a right bettor, took odds, and won the free-odds bet, he or she gets back $20 plus the original wager, having taken the odds at 2 to 1.

The use of free odds by a don't-pass bettor is as valid as

taking free odds when betting right. The payoffs are less, but they are still at the correct odds because, in our previous example, the chances of making the 4 before the 7 comes up are 2 to 1 against, therefore the wrong bettor is laying the exact and correct odds against the 4.

When laying odds against the point numbers, the free-odds bet allowed is always determined by the *payoff*, not the original don't-pass bet. For example, when single odds are allowed, and the don't-pass bettor has wagered $10 on the line, this player is permitted to lay $20 as the free-odds bet, since the payoff is at 1 to 2, and if the player wins the $20 free-odds bet, he or she collects a payoff of only $10.

Table 2 makes this concept absolutely clear by showing just how much a don't-pass bettor has to wager behind the line against each of the point numbers if the original don't-pass wager is $10.

TABLE 2

Number	Don't-Pass Wager	Free-Odds Bet
6 or 8	$10	$12 at 6 to 5
5 or 9	$10	$15 at 3 to 2
4 or 10	$10	$20 at 2 to 1

Each of these free-odds bets is laid, not taken, at the correct odds. Should a player win any of these bets, no matter what the point number, the payoff is always $20 plus the original bet. To explain further: After 6 or 8 was established as a point, the don't-pass player has bet a total of $22 against that number, $10 on don't pass and $12 on free odds. If the player wins the bet, he or she gets back $42, which represents $20 in winning and $22 for the original bet.

If the point was 5 or 9 and the wrong bettor won, the payoff is $45: $20 as winnings and $25 representing the original bet. And if the point was 4 or 10, the player gets back $50: $20 as winnings and $30 for the original bet.

For this reason, many players don't like to bet the "don't" side of the table, because they don't like to put out more chips on free odds than they get back as winnings if their bet wins. But, as mentioned before, the house has no advantage when the player lays the odds, and it's a good bet to make.

If you bet $5 on the line as a don't-pass wager, you can easily bet $6 as a free-odds bet, laying 6 for 5. If the point is 4 or 10, you can lay $10 behind the line, at 2 to 1 odds. But if the point is 5 or 9, the correct odds are 3 to 2, and the casino will not permit half-dollars to be bet, so there's no way to lay the correct 7½ to 5. However, the casino permits you to bet $9 behind the line as a free-odds wager against the 5 or 9, and if you win, you collect $6.

In fact, whenever the point is 5 or 9, and you've made an unequal don't-pass bet, you are permitted to wager a little more as a free-odds bet. Ask the dealer just how much you can bet, for the rules vary slightly from casino to casino in this regard.

Thus far, we've discussed single-odds games. In casinos where double odds are permitted, the same general rules apply. You can bet *double the payoff* as a free-odds bet, not double the line wager. Table 3 shows how this is done with basic $10 don't-pass bets.

TABLE 3

Number	Don't-Pass Wager	Free-Odds Bet
6 or 8	$10	$24 at 6 to 5
5 or 9	$10	$30 at 3 to 2
4 or 10	$10	$40 at 2 to 1

As you can see from Table 3, the wrong bettor is putting out quite a bit of money as free-odds bets when laying double odds against the point. For this reason, few players bet the full double odds when betting wrong, and it is our opinion that, even though double odds reduce the house edge fractionally, from 0.8 percent to 0.6 percent, you are better off in the long run just betting single odds against the point.

In fact, our strategies involving wrong betting suggest laying single odds against the numbers, for reasons dealing with the preservation of our bankroll at the table. When you lay double odds, a few repeating numbers can really hurt your bankroll.

The casino has a 1.4 percent edge over the wrong bettor who bets don't pass without laying odds. This figure is reduced to 0.8 percent when single odds are laid, and is further reduced to 0.6 percent when double odds are laid.

When laying free odds after a don't-pass bet, don't put the chips behind the original chips as you do when betting pass line, because the don't-pass area is much smaller. Put the chips representing the free-odds bet either next to the original chips or on the original chips at a slight tilt to differentiate them from the original bet. If in doubt, ask the dealer, who will show you how it's done.

If betting wrong, don't be afraid to lay those free odds; it's definitely to your advantage to do so in the long run. Don't worry about the smaller payoffs, because they are correct payoffs, since once a point is established, you have the advantage on the bet. Remember a 7 can be made in six combinations, and there's no point number that can be made in as many ways.

Like the free-odds bets made on pass-line wagers, the free-odds bets laid against the numbers can be removed or reduced at any time, but, again, our advice is never to do this because the house has no advantage on any of these free-odds bets.

FREE ODDS: DON'T COME

The don't-come wager is fully explained in the next chapter. It is the same as the don't pass, except that it can be bet only *after* the come-out roll, not prior to it. The same rules apply as with don't-pass wagers, and free odds can be laid against any of the numbers when betting the don't come.

After a come number is established, your don't-come bet is taken from the don't-come box by the dealer and put in an area behind (above) the appropriate place-number box. After this is done, you can give the dealer chips to lay the odds against the number just established. Simply say, "Odds on the don't" and the dealer puts the chips next to or on top of the original don't-come bet at a slight tilt.

If single odds are permitted, you can wager the equivalent of the payoff as your odds bet, and if double odds are allowed, you may wager double the payoff as your odds bet. As with all free-odds bets, they may be taken down or reduced at any time by the player, but this should not be done, for the house has no advantage on these wagers, and they reduce the overall house edge on don't-come bets.

VI

COME AND
DON'T-COME BETS

Of all the bets on the layout, the come and don't-come bets give players the most trouble, and many long time craps players avoid these wagers because they don't quite understand them and never play anything but line bets.

The come and don't-come bets are really not that difficult to understand or to make, and they are very worthwhile to any basic system or strategy for making money at the craps table. After you read the next few sections, you should have no problems with these bets, and once you understand them you'll be able to take full advantage of these wagers.

COME BETS

Come bets are made by right bettors and, therefore, are made much more often than don't-come bets because at least 90 percent of the craps players bet right. These players bet pass line, and many of them follow through with come bets, because come bets are identical to pass-line wagers, except for one thing: A pass-line bet can be made only *prior* to the come-out roll, whereas a come bet can be made only *after* a point is established.

Come and Don't-Come Bets

To refresh our memory, the most simple definition of a come-out roll is any roll made before a point is established. At the craps table, you can determine if there is a come-out roll about to begin. All you have to do is look at the marker puck each dealer controls. If it's resting on its black, or "Off," side in the don't-come box, then the next roll is a come-out roll. However, if the puck is on its white, or "On," side and resting in a place-number box, in the 4, 5, 6, 8, 9, or 10, then that number is the point that has already been established, and you can make come bets.

To make the come bet, put your chip or chips in the betting area marked "Come" on the layout. The next roll of the dice affects your bet, and the bet is governed by the same rules that apply to the pass-line wager.

• If a 7 or 11 is rolled, you have an immediate winner, paid off at even money.

• If a 2, 3, or 12 is thrown, you lose your wager immediately.

• If a point number, now called a come number, 4, 5, 6, 8, 9, or 10 is rolled, this number must be repeated before a 7 is thrown for you to win your come bet.

• Should a come number be thrown, and a 7 is rolled before that number is repeated, you lose your bet.

After a come number is established, the chips are removed by the dealer from the come box and put in the appropriate place-number box, in a designated area in the box.

After a come number is established, you may make a free-odds bet on that number, in the same manner as if it were a pass-line wager. The only difference in making the bet is that you hand your chips to the dealer and tell him to make the odds bet, rather than doing it yourself.

When you make come bets, it means that you must follow more than one number, but the dealer helps you out, and it's not that difficult, really. The dealer has been trained to keep track of all players' bets and will inform you about any wins or losses on the come bets.

When you're at the table, you can easily follow your own come bets. They are handled by the dealer on your side of the table, and since few players make this wager, you can simply look at each place-number box for the bets you've already established as come numbers.

Come bets are very worthwhile when a hot roll develops, one in which many numbers repeat, for you're not limited to one come bet but can make as many as you want, as long as the same shooter holds the dice and the point is still alive.

There have been instances where I have seen the shooter hold the dice for almost three-quarters of an hour without making the point. All the while the lucky shooter was rolling numbers, 4, 5, 6, 8, and 9 (the point was 10), and players who simply had made only a pass-line wager did not reap the benefits of those repeating numbers the way the come bettors were.

Remember, after you make your come bet and a come number is rolled, you win if that number is repeated. If you've been wise enough to take free odds on that number, you'll be paid off at correct odds for the free-odds wager as well. So, to maximize your profits at the craps table, always take advantage of the come bets.

Let's follow a shoot to see how the come bet works in practice. You'll be betting pass line and then making continuous come bets, all at $10, in a single-odds casino. Of course, you'll take the maximum odds permitted at all times on all your bets.

Roll	Number	Bets and Results
Come Out	5	$10 on pass line and $10 odds

On the come out you could make only a pass-line wager. The point is 5, and the puck is moved to the 5 place-number box. You can now make come bets, so you place $10 in chips in the come box.

46

Come and Don't-Come Bets

First Come   6 $10 and $10 odds

After the 6 was rolled, the dealer took your chips and put them in the place-number box 6. Once the chips are placed there, you can make an odds bet, and so you give the dealer $10 and tell him "odds." The dealer puts your chips on the original come bet at an offset. In the same manner, after every $10 come bet is established, hand the dealer an additional $10 in chips as an odds bet on that number.

Second Come   12 $10 loss

The 12, a craps, is a losing bet on the come, and so you now put an additional $10 into the come box.

Third Come   10 $10 and $10 odds

After each roll, put $10 into the come box for the next come bet.

Fourth Come   11 $10 win

You immediately win $10 on the come bet, because an 11 is a winner, just as it is on the pass line.

Fifth Come   5 $10 and $10 odds
$25 win on point 5

The 5, by repeating, made you a winner on the pass-line bet. But the 5 was a come number as well, and you had to give the dealer an additional $10 to make certain that you had an odds bet on the 5.

At this time, there's a new come-out roll. Looking over the layout, you see that you have three numbers working for you as come numbers; the 6, 10, and 5.

You can't make a come bet now, because it's a new come-out roll, and only pass-line wagers can be made prior to this roll. You put $10 on the pass line.

We should now talk about the come numbers. Come numbers are always working, that is, they're always subject to the next roll of the dice, even on the come-out roll, although they can't bet on the come-out roll.

However, even though the come bets are always working, the free-odds bets on these come numbers are "off" on the come-out roll; that is, they're not subject to the come-out roll. If any of the come numbers were rolled on the come out, either a 6, 10, or 5, you would win $10 for the come bet, but not anything on the odds bet since they're "off." The odds bets would be returned to you on that particular number.

On the other hand, if 7 were rolled, all the come numbers already established, the 6, 10, and 5, would be losers, except for the odds, because the 7 showed before any of those numbers repeated. You would lose $30 on the come bets on all three numbers, but would retain the free-odds bets on these numbers. They would be returned to you. This procedure applies only on the come-out roll, not after that. After the new point is established the come and free-odds bets are both working and subject to the next roll of the dice. The following two shoots will show this.

Roll	Number	Bets and Results
Come Out	4	$10 on pass line and $10 odds
First Come	6	$10 and $10 odds
Second Come	4	$30 win on point 4
		$10 and $10 odds

There's a new come-out roll now, with the player having the 6 and 4 established as come numbers.

New Come Out	6	$10 and $10 odds
		$10 win on come 6

48

The player won only $10 because the odds bet on the come numbers were off on the come-out roll. The $10 bet on free odds on the 6 as a come number are returned to him. At this time, the new point is 6, and the player has only one come number, 4, working, because 6, when it showed on the come-out roll, not only made the 6 a come-number win, but caused it to be taken down by the dealer.

The next shoot covers other situations.

Roll	*Number*	*Bets and Results*
Come Out	5	$10 on pass line and $10 odds
First Come	8	$10 and $10 odds
Second Come	8	$22 win on come 8
		$10 and $10 odds

The 8 repeated as a come number and was a winning bet for the bettor. He collected both his original and free-odds bet on this number because it repeated in the course of the shoot, not on the come-out roll. And it wasn't taken down, but re-established as a come number for the same reason. Now the player has 5 as his point and 8 as his come number. The roll continues:

Third Come	5	$25 win on point 5
		$10 and $10 odds

There is now a new come-out roll, since the point was repeated. At this time, the player has two come numbers working for him: 8 and 5.

New Come Out	7	$10 win on pass line
		$10 loss on come 8
		$10 loss on come 5

The roll of a 7 on the come out is a winner for the pass-line bet, but it loses both previously established come bets,

49

the 8 and 5, since a 7 showed on the dice before any of these numbers repeated. However, only the come bets and not the free-odds bets were lost because 7 came up on the come-out roll, and all free-odds bets on come numbers are off on the come-out roll.

Although the standard rules of casino craps are that the free-odds bets are off on the come-out roll, a come bettor may ask the dealer to leave them on, and working all the time. In practically all casinos this can be done, and then if a 7 is rolled on the come out not only the come bets but the free-odds bets on the come numbers would be lost. On the other hand, if a come number repeated on the come-out roll, the player would be paid off for both the come bet and the additional free-odds bet, at correct odds.

Come bets may be made continuously, as we have seen, and in varying sizes. We had bet a standard $10 each time, but each come bet may vary in size, according to the wishes of the players. They are bound only by the house minimum and maximum limits. For example, a player may bet $50 on the first come wager, $500 on the next, $30 on the next, and $5 on the next one. Of course, when this is done, there is no rhyme or reason to the betting, but it could be done if the player wanted to bet that way.

Come bets, once established, cannot be reduced or removed, but the free-odds bets on these come wagers can always be taken down or reduced, but never should be, for as we have said so many times before, the house has no advantage on these bets, and they reduce the casino edge overall.

The same odds that affect pass-line bets affect come bets. The house has a 1.41 percent edge on come bets made without odds taken, 0.8 percent when come bets are made with single odds, and 0.6 percent when double odds are taken.

DON'T-COME BETS

These bets, like come wagers, can be made only after a point has been established. If in doubt, either ask the dealer when you first come to a table, or look for the marker puck each dealer controls. If it's on its white side and resting in a place-number box, you can make don't-come bets.

Once you have actively participated in the game, there will be no problem. You can make your don't-come bet after you've made a don't-pass wager and a point has been established.

Don't-come bets are governed by the same rules as don't-pass bets, and these are:

• A roll of a 2 or 3 is an immediate winner, paid off at even money.

• A 12 is a standoff, except in casinos where the 2 is barred and then the roll of a 2 is a standoff, while the 3 and 12 become immediate winners.

• The throw of a 7 or 11 is an immediate loser.

• If a point number, now called a come number—4, 5, 6, 8, 9, or 10—is rolled, and a 7 comes up before that number is repeated, the don't-come bettor wins.

• If the come number repeats before a 7 is thrown, the don't-come player loses.

• Free odds may be laid against any come number when betting the don't come. Where single odds are permitted, single odds may be laid against the payoff, and where double odds are allowed, double odds may be laid against the payoff.

To make a don't-come bet, place your chip or chips in the don't-come box. If a come number is next rolled, your chips are taken by the dealer and placed behind (or above) the appropriate place-number box. You can look at the layout to verify this position.

After your don't-come bet has been placed, you can give the dealer additional chips for a free-odds wager against the number. You are laying odds in all cases, when betting the don't come.

The odds laid are the same as with don't-pass wagers. You lay 6 to 5 against the 6 or 8, 3 to 2 against the 5 or 9, and 2 to 1 against the 4 or 10.

Let's assume that you've put $10 in the don't-come box and the next roll of the dice is 4. The dealer takes the chips from the don't-come box and puts them behind the appropriate place-number box so that he knows you have a don't-come bet against the 4. Next, you can give him $20 in chips as a free-odds bet at 2 to 1 against the 4. If the 7 shows before the 4 repeats, you win $10 on your original bet and $10 for your free-odds bet, for a total win of $20. Should you lose your bets, you'd lose the full $30.

A wrong bettor can make continuous don't-come wagers, as many and in whatever denominations the player desires, governed only by the house minimum and maximum betting limits. And the bettor can lay free odds on all his or her don't-come wagers.

Don't-come bets, like come bets, are always working, even on the come-out roll. However, unlike come bets, don't-come free-odds bets are also always working and are never off, not even on the come-out roll.

Therefore, every roll of the dice potentially affects your don't-come bets and your free-odds bets as well, which is not the case when come bets are made.

Unlike come bettors, who fear the 7, since it wipes out all their previously established come numbers and loses all their bets, the wrong bettor wagering on don't come is always hoping for the 7 to show on the dice, since it makes all his previous bets winners. To illustrate this, we'll follow one shoot. You, the wrong bettor, are betting $10 and laying single odds on the don't pass, making continuous don't-come bets thereafter, and also laying single odds against the come numbers.

Come and Don't-Come Bets

Roll	Number	Bets and Results
Come Out	5	$10 on don't pass and $15 odds
First Come	8	$10 and $12 odds
Second Come	4	$10 and $20 odds
Third Come	6	$10 and $12 odds
Fourth Come	7	$10 loss on don't-come bet
		$20 win on point 5
		$20 win on come 8
		$20 win on come 4
		$20 win on come 6
Total Wins		$80
Total Losses		$10
Net Win		$70

The fourth come bet in the above shoot was a losing one for the don't-come bettor because the 7 showing on any roll is a losing roll for a don't-come player. But since the 7 came up before any of the other numbers repeated, they became all winning bets for the don't-come bettor.

The next shoot illustrates how the don't-come bet and free-odds bets on the numbers are always working, even on the come-out roll.

Roll	Number	Bets and Results
Come Out	10	$10 on don't pass and $20 odds
First Come	4	$10 and $20 odds
Second Come	6	$10 and $12 odds
Third Come	8	$10 and $12 odds
Fourth Come	9	$10 and $15 odds
Fifth Come	10	$30 loss on point 10
		$10 and $20 odds

Now there is a new come-out roll since the point, 10, repeated and was made.

New Come Out	7	$10 loss on don't pass
		$20 win on come 4
		$20 win on come 6
		$20 win on come 8
		$20 win on come 9
		$20 win on come 10

Total Wins	$100
Total Losses	$ 40
Net Win	$ 60

As can be seen from the above shoot, the 7 is the great benefactor of the don't-come bettor. Unlike the come bettor, who can lose all bets with the single roll of a 7, the don't-come bettor can only lose his or her bets one at a time, as numbers repeat. But if enough repeat, the don't-come player can take a real beating.

VII

PLACE BETS AND PLACE NUMBERS

PLACE BETS

The area devoted to place numbers on the layout is rather large, showing individual boxes where the bets are put after they're made. The place numbers are the same as point numbers: 4, 5, 6, 8, 9, and 10. They may be bet individually, in groups, or all at once by any player.

When a player makes a place bet on one or more of these numbers, he or she is betting that the number or numbers will come up before the shooter sevens-out. Thus, these bets are off on the come-out roll, and are working only after a point has been established. However, players can call place bets "on" on the come out.

Instead of betting a series of come bets, the place bettor can immediately cover as many numbers as desired, and get paid off as soon as they come up. Of course, if the shooter sevens-out, the place bettor loses all the place bets at once.

The place bet is the mainstay of the casino's profits at the craps table, for it is an extremely popular one with right bettors, who are impatient and want to have action on every roll of the dice. Betting the place numbers is the fastest way to maximize profits at the craps table, but it has inherent risks and betting the place numbers indiscriminately makes a player an outright gambler rather than an astute bettor.

There are two basic reasons for the popularity of the place bets.

First, they are unaffected by the come-out roll, being off on that roll. If there is a long, hot hand held by a shooter, in which many points and repeat numbers are made, the place bettors can reap a fortune. In this regard, they have an advantage over the come bettors.

During a long shoot, the shooter may roll a couple of 7s on the come-out roll, which, although winners on the pass line, lose all come bets for those wagering and establishing come numbers, since come bets are always working, even on the come-out roll. The place bettor's wagers are immune from these 7s on the come-out roll, however, and this player does not constantly have to re-establish bets after a 7 shows on the come out.

Second, unlike come bets, the place bettor is paid off immediately once a number bet on shows on the dice, whereas a come bettor has to wait for that number to repeat before being paid off. If the place bettor has covered the number 5 with $10, and on the first come roll the number is 5, the place bettor is an immediate winner, getting paid $14, while the come bettor would be first establishing the number 5 on a come bet.

In these two ways, place numbers are much more attractive than come numbers, and I would heartily recommend them as attractive bets, except for one factor that rears its ugly head: that is the house edge on place bets. The house edge on these wagers is much higher than on come bets, especially when come bets are enhanced with free-odds bets as well. The casinos, recognizing the attractiveness and popularity of place bets to right bettors, have structured them so that they give the house an inordinate advantage over the player.

Place Bets and Place Numbers

Table 1 shows the correct odds against any of the place numbers being made, the house payoff on these numbers as place bets, and the resulting house advantage.

TABLE 1

Numbers	Correct Odds Against	House Payoff on Place Bets	Casino Advantage
4 and 10	2 to 1	9 to 5	6.67%
5 and 9	3 to 2	7 to 5	4.0%
6 and 8	6 to 5	7 to 6	1.52%

As can readily be seen, the house edge is higher than the advantage it enjoys on come bets, which is only 1.41 percent. And when the come bettor makes additional free-odds wagers the edge drops to 0.8 percent with single odds, 0.6 percent with double odds. This compares favorably with the 1.52 percent, 4 percent, and 6.67 percent advantage the house has on place bets.

That's basically the trouble with place bets. The player, in order to get instant payoffs, must give the house too much of an advantage on most of these wagers. In fact, the advantage the house has is so great on the 4, 5, 9, and 10 that we never recommend these numbers be covered as place bets. Only the 6 and 8 are worthwhile under certain circumstances, and these will be shown in conjunction with some of the betting methods we recommend.

Let us go into the mechanics of place bets to make their process absolutely clear. You may cover the place numbers by betting on them after the come-out roll.

Because of the fixed payoffs at either 7 to 5 or 9 to 5 on the 4, 5, 9, and 10, known as the "outside numbers," in order to get the proper house odds offered on these wagers, you would have to bet at least $5 on any of these numbers in practically all casinos. For purposes of this book, we're excluding the few "quarter joints" that allow 25¢ bets. We are excluding 25¢ casinos because readers playing in Atlantic City, in many other jurisdictions, and in the better clubs won't be able to make bets in 25¢ amounts. If a player wants to play in 25¢ casinos, fine. But we're structuring this book for bettors who can wager at least $5 on the place numbers.

Any wager on the above numbers at less than $5 would be paid off at even money, giving the house a monstrous edge on these bets, and any bets not made in multiples of $5 would accomplish the same poor result. For example, you put $9 on the place number 4, and if it comes up, you'd be paid back 9 to 5 on the first $5 but only even money on the remaining $4 you bet.

Any competent dealer will direct you to make the proper bets on these numbers. If a dealer is given $9 to wager on the 4, he should inform you that $10 is required to get the proper 9 to 5 payoff. I'm using the word "proper" rather than "correct," for the correct payoff would be at 2 to 1.

When wagering on 6 and 8, since the payoff is 7 to 6, you should wager at least $6 or multiples thereof, to ensure getting the proper payoff at 7 to 6. Again, we are excluding the few casinos that permit 25¢ wagers.

You are now ready to make your place bets after the come-out roll, and here's how it's done. First, you cannot put your chips into the place-number boxes yourself; only the dealer can do this, and so you must give your chips to the dealer and tell him exactly what numbers you want bet and in what amounts.

A standard way to do this (however, we don't recommend it, but are just explaining it) is to cover all the numbers except the point number, which we assume, has already been covered by a pass-line wager.

For example, suppose that the point is 6, and the player has bet $10 on the pass line. If he or she wants similar bets to cover the place numbers, the player gives the dealer $52 and says "cover all the numbers," or "across the board," or words to that effect, directing the dealer to place the chips on the remaining open place numbers, other than the 6.

The chips, as mentioned earlier, must be given to the dealer. There are several reasons for this procedure. The place boxes are too far away to be conveniently reached by the players, and the dealer may have several place bets working at one time from chips given to him by other players, and he positions the chips so that he can pay off each bettor in proper order.

When the dealer gets the $52, he puts $10 each on the horizontal lines in front of the 4, 5, 9, and 10 place-number boxes, and $12 on the place number 8. The bet is $12 on the 8, because the payoff is 7 to 6, and a $10 wager on the 8 is an improper one as far as a payoff is concerned.

When the point is other than a 6 or 8, a $10 bettor wanting to cover all the numbers other than the point gives the dealer $2 more, or $54. This is because the 6 and 8 place numbers take $12 apiece, adding $2 to the total cost of covering all place numbers.

Some players bet all the place numbers including the point number, but this is an extremely bad practice, for a pass-line bet gives the house only 1.41 percent without odds, while any of the other place bets are at even more of a disadvantage to the player.

Although we have shown across-the-board wagering covering all the numbers, bettors may make all kinds of different bets on place numbers at amounts ranging from the house minimum of $5 all the way up to the maximum, usually $500 or $1,000, depending on the casino.

Therefore, a player may give a dealer $500 to wager on place number 5 and $100 to bet on place number 4, if desired. There need be no consistency in place bets. Certain numbers may be bet heavily, while others may be excluded altogether. For example, a player may bet $100 on 4, $200 on 10, $500 on 5, $250 on 9, and $6 each on 6 and 8. The place bettor can do anything within the minimum and maximum limits, creating any crazy-quilt betting pattern he or she wishes.

Some gamblers are superstitious and prefer one number or a group of numbers over others. Recently at a craps table in Atlantic City I watched a man bet $500 on place number 9, to the exclusion of any other bet on the layout. During the time I watched the play at the table, one 9 came up while eight 7s were rolled. But he persisted in his love affair with the 9.

Some players bet only the "outside numbers": 4, 5, 9, and 10, the worst bets as far as odds are concerned. Others bet only the inside numbers: 5, 6, 8, and 9.

Most place bettors like to cover all the numbers in a fixed pattern immediately after the point is established. This practice is very dangerous because a 7 thrown on the next roll wipes out these bets. Sometimes at a "cold" table, where 7s come up right after the point is established, a whole tableful of players can go broke in a short time if they persist in covering all the place numbers.

Another great advantage of place bets, which doesn't change the odds or the house advantage, however, is that these wagers can be removed, reduced, or increased at any time prior to the next roll of the dice.

When these bets are increased, many players like to "press their bets," or double their previous wager, on a number when it comes up. For example, if a player has $10 on the 5 and it is rolled, instead of collecting the entire $14 profit at 7 to 5, the player will tell the dealer to "press" the bet. The dealer makes the 5 a $20 bet and returns only $4 to the player as profit. Some players think the sky is the limit and keep pressing their bets, collecting little in the way of profits, and then the shooter sevens-out, while they lose their entire bet. This is a foolish and dangerous way to try and make a big win in a short time because no one knows when the 7 will come up on the dice and destroy all the place bets in one fell swoop.

If a player wishes to stop betting on the place numbers after a number of these bets are established, he or she can instruct the dealer that the place bets are "off" for one or more rolls, or until the dealer is told they're "working" again.

I've seen a player call off his $500 and $600 place bets on all the numbers for fourteen rolls of the dice, during which time every roll was a winning number, which would have made him about $7,000 in profits. Then, on a hunch, he called his bets "on" again, and the next roll of the dice was a losing one, a 7, and all his chips were taken away by the dealer.

No one can forecast the next roll of the dice, or how long they'll come up without the 7 showing. What intelligent players can do is understand the correct odds on the various bets open to them, and give as little to the house as possible, by avoiding foolish wagers; and place bets on the 4, 5, 9, and 10 are foolish bets.

Some players want place bets to be working all the time, even on the come-out roll. Most casinos go along with this request, but doing this takes away one of the advantages of place numbers: the fact that a 7 rolled on the come out does not affect them or remove them when they're "off."

How do we suggest betting place numbers? First, only the 6 and 8 should be bet on, giving the house just 1.52 percent as their edge. Then we suggest that you incorporate these bets into a betting strategy recommended in our section on winning methods of play for right bettors.

Otherwise, avoid indiscriminate place betting. They are not only bad bets from the point of view of the large casino edge, but they can seriously endanger your bankroll if a succession of 7s comes up right after the come-out roll. They are perhaps the quickest destroyers of bankrolls on the craps table.

BUYING THE 4 AND 10

The casino gives you the option of buying any place number, but it is only a worthwhile bet, relatively speaking, when buying the 4 and 10. To buy a number, you have to pay a 5 percent commission, and since the house edge on the 5 and 9 is 4 percent and the casino advantage on the 6 and 8 is only 1.52 percent, there's no purpose in buying these numbers.

However, by buying the 4 and 10, you're reducing the house edge from 6.67 percent to 4.76 percent, which is a substantial savings.

To buy either or both numbers, give the dealer the correct amount of chips plus an extra 5 percent commission. For example, if you bought the 4 for $20, the commission would be $1, or 5 percent of the $20. If you bought both the 4 and 10 for $20 apiece, you'd give the dealer $2 as the casino's commission. This commission is called the casino "vig," which is a short term for the slang word "vigorish" or edge.

Some casinos allow you to make a $25 bet and pay only $1 as vig. After you buy either or both numbers, the dealer puts a "buy" button on top of your chips to differentiate them from the normal place bets. Should your number come up, you are paid 2 to 1, the correct odds, instead of 9 to 5 paid on place numbers 4 and 10.

Thus, if you really want to cover the 4 and 10 as place numbers (something we don't advise), it would be foolish to bet them as place numbers. Your best bet is to buy them. If you bet $10 on one of these numbers, the house still extracts a $1 commission, so it pays to buy both the 4 and 10 at the same time for $20 and pay only a 5 percent commission or $1. If you're covering each number for $20, ask the dealer if you can bet $25 per number and still pay the $1 commission, for, if it's allowed, the house edge is reduced even further.

Thereafter, the rules of various casinos differ. Some pay you off at 2 to 1 and then ask for another dollar for every other bet; others do not. Some casinos keep your $1 commission if you decide to take down your bets; others refund the dollar if your numbers haven't come up and you decide to take them down.

Buy bets, like place wagers, can be taken down at any time, reduced, or increased before the next roll of the dice. If you increase your buy bet, you'll have to pay increased commissions, depending on how much you've raised it.

These buy bets do not work on the come-out roll, unless the player instructs the dealer that they're always on.

LAY WAGERS

Place bets are used by right bettors, those betting with the dice, hoping for numbers to show on the dice before a 7 is thrown. However, wrong bettors, those betting against the dice and desiring a fast 7 to show up on the dice, can bet against the numbers showing up by making lay wagers.

Unlike the place bettor, the player laying wagers must give the house an immediate 5 percent commission when making these bets. The commission is not determined by the bet, but by the payoff.

For instance, if you bet $40 against the 10, the commission you'd have to pay is $1, which represents 5 percent of the payoff of $20 if you win your bet. When laying bets, you'll be giving the casino the following advantages on your wagers:

Number	Casino Edge
4 and 10	2.44%
5 and 9	3.23%
6 and 8	4.0%

By betting this way, you leave yourself wide open to the numbers you wagered against coming up and thus wiping out your bets. Unlike don't-come bets, where the number must first be established and then repeated for you to lose your bet, here, an immediate throw of any of the numbers you bet against loses your bet.

Lay wagers, for that reason, are rarely made by players. For a player betting wrong, it would be much wiser to make don't-come bets, for not only are the odds better for you (0.8 percent when laying single odds) but the numbers would have to repeat before you lost your bet.

Lay wagers may be taken down, reduced, or increased at any time. If increased, additional commissions have to be paid to the casino.

VIII

OTHER LAYOUT BETS

FIELD BETS

Unlike the other wagers we've discussed so far, field bets are determined by the next roll of the dice, and thus are known as one-roll wagers.

By one-roll wager, we mean that the very next roll of the dice determines if you've won or lost your bet. You don't have to wait any longer than that for the result, and that is one of the appeals of the field bet, which is rarely made by astute players.

This bet is given a great deal of space on the craps layout, but the space is wasted, for only systems players, ignorant bettors, and others unfamiliar with the essential game of casino craps make this wager.

What also appeals to field bettors, besides the fact that they don't have to wait long for a result, is that there seem to be so many numbers that can make them winners, and very few that will cause them to lose their bet.

The field bet is essentially this: A player puts chips into the field-bet area, and should the next throw of the dice come up 2, 3, 4, 9, 10, 11, or 12, he or she wins the bet. In many casinos, if the 2 is thrown the player is paid off at 2 to

1, and if the 12 comes up on the next roll, the bettor gets 3 to 1 for the bet. If any of the other numbers displayed on the field bet come up, the win is paid off at even money.

However, should the 5, 6, 7, or 8, the four remaining numbers not shown on the layout, be rolled on the next throw of the dice, the player loses the bet. With all the numbers working for the player, plus the additional 2 to 1 payoff on the 2 and the 3 to 1 on the 12, it looks like a good bet to the unwary gambler not familiar with the odds of dice and the combinations that determine these odds.

Despite all the numbers that the players have going for them, the house does have an advantage over the gamblers on the field bet. This advantage may be either 2.70 percent when either the 2 or 12 is paid off at 3 to 1 while the other number is paid off at 2 to 1, or a 5.55 percent edge if both the 2 and 12 are paid off at 2 to 1.

Most of the downtown casinos in Las Vegas, as well as many clubs in northern Nevada, and all the casinos in Atlantic City pay off either the 2 or 12 at 3 to 1, giving these houses a 2.70 percent edge over the player. The Strip casinos in Las Vegas and certain other clubs in northern Nevada pay off both the 2 and 12 at 2 to 1, giving these casinos a 5.55 percent advantage over the field bettor.

We don't advise ever making a field bet. Many other bets on the layout give the house less of an edge over the bettor, and the way to win at casino craps is always to keep the casino advantage down to a minimum.

Table 1 shows how the odds on the field bet are calculated.

Table 2 shows the ways that the missing numbers can be made to determine the correct odds on this bet.

Since the missing numbers can be rolled in twenty ways, and the field numbers in only nineteen ways, the odds against the field bet is 20 to 19, giving the house an edge of 2.70 percent over the bettor. When both the 2 and 12 are paid off at 2 to 1 only, the odds change to 20 to 18

Other Layout Bets

TABLE 1

Field Number	Combinations	Ways Can Be Made
2	1–1 × 2 (2 to 1 payoff)	2
3	1–2, 2–1	2
4	1–3, 3–1, 2–2	3
9	3–6, 6–3, 4–5, 5–4	4
10	4–6, 6–4, 5–5	3
11	5–6, 6–5	2
12	6–6 × 3 (3 to 1 payoff)	3
	Total Ways	19

TABLE 2

Number	Combinations	Ways Can Be Made
5	1–4, 4–1, 2–3, 3–2	4
6	1–5, 5–1, 2–4, 4–2, 3–3	5
7	1–6, 6–1, 2–5, 5–2, 3–4, 4–3	6
8	2–6, 6–2, 3–5, 5–3, 4–4	5
	Total Ways	20

against the field bet, and the house edge moves up to 5.55 percent.

Because the field bet is a one-roll wager, determined by the very next throw of the dice, it's always working, even on the come-out roll.

You can make this wager by betting any amount from the house minimum to the house maximum, but again, we advise against making this bet.

If you feel you must make a field bet, at least make it where the house gives you the best chance, where the 2 or 12 is paid off at 3 to 1. Otherwise, resist all temptations to put your chips on the field bet.

BIG SIX AND BIG EIGHT

There is ample space on the layout for this bet, which is one of the worst that can be made by a player, except when made in the Atlantic City casinos, but we'll go into the reasons for this later. In all other casinos, other than those in Atlantic City, the house has a tremendous edge over the player, an advantage so great that only a fool would buck it.

Here's how the bet works: You put your chips in the Big Six or Big Eight box, or in both, for the odds are the same no matter how this bet is made. Should the 6 or 8 (whichever number you bet on) come up before a 7 shows on the dice, you win your bet at even money.

However, should the 7 come up first, you lose your bet. It's a very simple wager and that's why it appeals to many ignorant players. The rub is this: The 6 or 8 can be rolled only in five different ways. The 7 can be made in six different combinations. Therefore the odds against making either a 6 or 8 before a 7 shows is 6 to 5, giving the house a 9.09 percent edge over the player on this bet.

In practically all casinos, you can bet from the house minimum to the house maximum on this wager, but you should never make this bet, with but one exception, which is covered below.

In the Atlantic City casinos, the Big Six and Big Eight wagers are paid off at 7 to 6, the same as place bets, if the gambler bets $6 or multiples thereof. If the players bet odd amounts, they will be paid off only at even money.

For example, if a player puts down $10 on the Big Eight in one of the Atlantic City casinos, the payoff is 7 to 6 for the first $6 and even money for the other $4. Thus the odd $4 bet gives the house a 9.09 percent edge.

When the payoff is at 7 to 6, the house has only a 1.52 percent advantage, the exact edge it has on the place numbers 6 and 8. But, to make certain that you get this proper payoff, you must bet at least $6 and in multiples of $6 on the Big Six and Big Eight in Atlantic City.

Otherwise, avoid this bet. If you really want to cover the 6 and 8, bet them as place numbers if you're in a casino other than in Atlantic City, and bet them for at least $6 and, if wagering more, in multiples of $6.

IX

THE CENTER, OR PROPOSITION, BETS

All bets discussed in this chapter are under the control of the stickman and are placed and handled by him. The chips may be given to a standing dealer by the player to be put on a proposition bet, but they are eventually given to the stickman to place in the appropriate betting box.

There are a variety of bets in the center boxes, and if you examine that portion of the craps layout, you'll notice all the bets that can be made. We must advise you that *none of these wagers* should be made by any player. The odds against the bettor range from terrible to horrendous.

The following is the center of the craps layout:

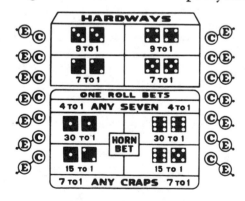

Nevada layout
Las Vegas, Nevada

Despite the fact that all these bets are bad, we'll discuss them one at a time to explain why they're no good. We'll begin with the one-roll wagers that can be made in the center of the layout.

ONE-ROLL CENTER BETS

To refresh our memories, a one-roll bet means that the next roll of the dice determines whether we win or lose our bet, and thus, one-roll bets are always working, for they are concerned with the very next toss of the dice.

Any Seven

Leading this group is the worst bet on the layout, a wager that is rarely made by any gambler. The bet is that the next roll of the dice will be a 7.

The bet is paid off at either 4 to 1 or 5 for 1, which is the same thing, because, in either case, you get back five chips for the one chip you bet.

Since there are only six ways to roll a 7 out of thirty-six possible combinations, the odds against a 7 showing on any particular roll of the dice is 5 to 1. By paying off at 4 to 1, the house has an advantage over the bettor of 16.67 percent.

There is no reason to ever make this bet.

Any Craps

This wager can be seen at the bottom of the center layout, and along the sides, in the circles marked with a "C," which stands for craps. It's a very popular bet with a great many players and gets a lot of action. What these gamblers are betting on when they make this wager is that the next roll of the dice will come up a "craps," that is, a 2, 3, or 12.

Most of the money wagered on this proposition bet is

made on the come-out roll, where a whole shower of chips will be thrown to the stickman by right bettors. Those gamblers who bet with the dice on the pass line feel they are "protecting" their line bets against a craps showing on the come-out roll, which, of course, is an immediate loser on the pass line. However, this kind of thinking is erroneous and misguided. The bet doesn't protect anything but the casino's bankroll, for it gives the house an edge of 11.1 percent over the player.

There are only four ways to roll all of the craps: two for the 3, and one each for the 2 and 12. Since there are thirty-six combinations on the dice, that leaves thirty-two ways this bet can lose. The correct odds are therefore 8 to 1 against a craps showing up on any particular roll of the dice, and since the house pays only 7 to 1 on this wager, the house advantage works out to 11.1 percent.

No matter how tempting this bet may be, no matter how many other players are making the wager, stay away from this bet and never make it.

The 2 or 12

You can bet that the next roll of the dice will come up 2, or you can wager that it will come up 12, and in either case, the house pays you 30 to 1 on your bet if you win.

However, we know that there are thirty-six possible combinations of dice, and each of these numbers can be made with only one combination, leaving the true odds at 35 to 1 against this occurring.

This gives the casino an advantage of 13.89 percent on this wager. Where casinos only pay 30 for 1, or 29 to 1, which is the same payoff, the house advantage rises to 16.67 percent.

Some wrong bettors make this wager on the come out, putting some chips on 12 or 2, whichever number is barred as a winning one on don't pass by the particular house. But, judging from the odds, we can see it's a foolish bet, and should never be made.

The 3 or 11

When you make this bet, you're wagering that the next roll of the dice will come up 3 (if you bet that number) or 11 (if you cover that number). There are only two ways to make either number out of thirty-six combinations on the dice and the odds against either a 3 or an 11 showing on any one roll of the dice are 17 to 1. The casino pays you only 15 to 1 on the bet, giving the house an advantage of 11.1 percent.

In casinos where the payoff is even less, 15 for 1, which really means 14 to 1, the house edge is 16.67 percent.

Never make this bet.

Horn Bet

This one-roll bet is seen in a number of casinos. You'll find it in Atlantic City and in northern Nevada for the most part, but don't search for it, for it's a useless wager.

It is a four-way bet, in which you wager that the next roll of the dice will be either a 2, 3, 11, or 12. Thus, four chips have to be placed on the horn bet.

The casino pays off this bet individually, according to the number rolled, and deducts the three losing chips. Since the payoff is at the usual house odds on each number already discussed in full, the house has a terrific edge over the player, and thus, this bet should never be made.

Hop Bet

This bet is not shown on the layout, but is allowed in many casinos. It's a one-roll wager in which the player picks a number that he or she feels will come up on the next roll of the dice and bets on it.

Generally speaking, the bet is usually made on a number not found in the center of the layout on the one-roll wagers we've already discussed. The gambler, when making a hop bet, looks for a more exotic bet, one that is not generally a one-roll wager. Thus, the player may bet on the hard 4, 2–2, coming up on the very next throw of the dice.

Hop bets such as this are paid off at 30 for 1, or 29 to 1, giving the house an advantage over the player of 16.67 percent.

The bet has to be sought out, since it's not on the layout, but don't bother. There's no reason to make such a bad bet —ever.

OTHER CENTER BETS

The Hardways

These are not one-roll wagers, but like all center bets, they're not worthwhile for the player. When making any hardway wagers, you're betting that the particular number you choose will come up hard before it comes up easy, or before a 7 is thrown. Let's first describe what a hardway is.

There are only four numbers that can be bet as hardways: 4, 6, 8, and 10. Each of these numbers are even numbers, of course, and each can be rolled as a pair. The 4 can be rolled as 2–2, the 6 as 3–3, the 8 as 4–4, and the 10 as 5–5. When any of these numbers is rolled as such a pair, it is said to be a hardway, or rolled "hard."

Should the numbers 4, 6, 8, or 10 be rolled in any other combinations, they are said to be rolled "easy" and are called "easy ways."

For example, a 4 rolled as 1–3, a 6 rolled as 5–1, an 8 rolled as 6–2, and a 10 rolled as 6–4 are all "easy ways."

Hard 4 and Hard 10

We can link these two numbers, for they are identical as far as the odds are concerned. Each can be rolled easy in two different ways. The 4 can be rolled 1–3 or 3–1, and the 10 as either 6–4 or 4–6. But the 7 can be rolled in six different ways.

Therefore, the odds against rolling a hard 4 or a hard 10 before it comes up easy or before 7 is thrown is 8 to 1. The casino pays off this bet at 7 to 1, and thus has an advantage of 11.1 percent on this wager.

Hard 6 and Hard 8

Again, these two numbers can be linked together, because the chances of rolling either as a hardway before it comes up easy or before a 7 is thrown are identical.

A 6 can be rolled easy in four different ways, as 1–5, 5–1, 2–4, and 4–2. An 8 can also be rolled easy in four ways: 2–6, 6–2, 3–5, 5–3. But a 7 can be thrown in six different ways.

Therefore, the odds against rolling either a hard 6 or hard 8 before they come up easy or before 7 shows on the dice is 10 to 1. The casino pays off this bet at 9 to 1, and has an edge of 9.09 percent on this wager.

There is no reason ever to make any kind of hardway bet.

X

WINNING METHODS OF PLAY: RIGHT BETTORS

This chapter covers several methods of play, running from the basic and conservative to the best-planned aggressive strategies. Within this framework, we'll be giving the house the absolute minimum edge possible in the game, at the same time working out a method of betting that allows us to make large profits.

As the methods get more aggressive, the house edge increases in some instances, but it is a slight increase at most, for none of the methods outlined will put the player in a position of bucking an outrageous house edge. The methods include several for wrong, or don't, bettors as well as for pass-line, or right, bettors.

All of the methods and strategies have been tested time and time again in actual casino play. They work because, although they give the casino a nominal edge, they call for a progressive betting system when the dice are going your way and your way only. Casino managers fear these increased betting methods most of all, because they know that one hot roll can really hurt them if players raise their bets when they are winning.

On the other hand, the casino executives always welcome "systems players" with open arms, but what the casino personnel considers a system is not what we're going to discuss with these betting methods. Most systems players hope for one individual win after losses, and their methods involve increasing bets only *after losses*, so that one final win allows them to either break even or show a slight profit.

These types of progressive systems, which include the Martingale and d'Alembert systems, eventually lead to ruin, and have been shown to be mathematically unsound. In actual play, these doubling and cancellation methods of betting can prove ruinous.

Our methods don't involve this kind of absurd betting scheme. We're always thinking of really hurting the casino, of making a fortune for you with one favorable roll, and, therefore, our methods are aimed at increases of bets only *after previous wins*. If we've lost the previous bet, as you shall see, our bets remain the same or decrease in certain instances.

But should that hot or favorable roll come, then you're going to make a big win. With our methods a $5 bettor can quickly escalate to $25 bets and beyond, and a high roller, in the $25- and $100-chip category, can ruin a casino's profit picture for a long time.

When we discuss betting strategies, we'll always be dealing in units rather than chip denominations. For example, we mean *three betting units*, rather than $15 for three $5 chips or $75 for $25 chips.

On occasion, however, in showing the profitable examples resulting from our methods, we'll revert to dollar denominations to make this perfectly clear. But you should know that, whether you bet with $1, $5, $25, or $100 chips, the principles remain the same, and you'll be a winner.

RIGHT BETTORS: THE BASIC METHOD, SINGLE ODDS

The basic method we are outlining in this section is the very best way to bet in casino craps when you're a right bettor. While it's not the most aggressive, or the most conservative, it's the safest, nonetheless, and it can lead to huge profits despite its safety.

This is the method the dealers call the "tough" one, for they know that anyone who has mastered and played it is a "tough player," a bettor who can hurt the casino and who is tough to beat.

This method takes into consideration two factors: first, playing it gives the house its lowest possible edge; second, it allows the player, through multiple and increased bets, to net a large profit if the dice go the player's way.

This method, and all others presented in this book, can be played in casinos that allow single or double odds at their tables. The betting arrangement is slightly different for each kind of game and will therefore be discussed separately.

One final bit of advice before we go into the right bettor's basic method thoroughly. If you can play at a double-odds casino, always play there. This is possible in Las Vegas, in certain casinos both downtown and on the Strip, and in many of the Reno clubs. In Atlantic City, all craps games feature single odds only.

The following are the steps necessary to bet this method. It's a simple one, easily understood and put into play, and yet it is very effective.

• First, make a three-unit bet on the pass line. The bet can be a $3, $15, $75, or $300 bet, but make sure to bet three units. There's a definite reason for this. If you bet three units, the casino allows you to bet four units as a free-odds bet if the point is 5 or 9, and five units if the point is 6 or 8. And this policy goes for come bets as well. You're not restricted to a $15 or a $75 bet using three units. You can bet $30 on the pass line and it will serve the same purpose, or $60 or $90, any units that are divisible by three. For instance, a $60 bet consists of three units of $20 each. This factor should be your basic guide in determining your bets.

• After the point is established, back up the line bet with as much as you can in free odds. If the point is 4 or 10, you're allowed to bet only three units behind the line as a free-odds bet. With 5 or 9 you can bet four units behind the line, and you can place five units as a free-odds bet if the point is 6 or 8.

• Next, make a come bet of the same three units by putting your chips into the come box. After a come number is established, give the dealer the maximum number of chips allowed for a single-odds bet.

• Make another come bet of three units by placing additional chips in the come box. After that come number is established, give the dealer the maximum free odds allowed.

• After two come bets are established, stop betting. It may take several come rolls for this to occur, because the 2, 3, 11, or 12 may be thrown on these rolls. After you collect or lose come wagers because of these numbers, keep betting the come wager. You must establish two come numbers before you stop making bets. The same principle holds true in the event that a come number repeats. You'll be paid off on the previous winning come bet, but you have to keep making bets to get two come numbers established.

Let's follow a sample shoot to see how all this works. The bets will be $15 at all times, and you'll back up all your wagers with free odds.

Roll	Number	Bets and Results
Come Out	8	$15 on pass line and $25 odds (five units)
First Come	5	$15 and $20 odds (four units)
Second Come	5	$45 win on come 5 $15 and $20 odds

We must make another come bet because only one come number, the 5, has been established.

Third Come	12	$15 loss
Fourth Come	11	$15 win
Fifth Come	4	$15 and $15 odds

In the above shoot, it took five come rolls to establish the two come numbers. We have stopped betting at this time because we don't want to be greedy, for greed is the ultimate leveler of all craps players. We are satisfied to have three numbers working for us: the point and two come numbers. Even if a 7 were now rolled, and we lose all our previous bets, we can withstand the loss.

The one problem that may occur is when a point number repeats before our two come numbers are established. In that event, we make another pass-line bet on the come-out roll, and after the point is established, we then make enough come bets to establish our two come numbers.

What should always be borne in mind is this: In using this betting method, we're endeavoring to establish three working numbers; one pass-line and two come numbers. No matter what interruptions occur, either favorable or unfavorable, we keep betting until those three numbers are working for us. Then we stop betting.

BASIC METHOD WITH INCREASED BETS, SINGLE ODDS

By increasing our bets after each win, we're going to put ourselves in a position to really win a lot of money. In showing the basic method in the previous section, we stay with the same bets all the time. But we're going to increase our wagers after each win, so that, with a moderately hot roll, we can take away a big profit from the craps table.

Again, we begin with the same basic three-unit bet, but from now on, whenever we have a winning bet, either on the pass line or come, we'll increase our bet. This increase can be one, two, or three units. Any increase will take advantage of a favorable series of rolls. However, we prefer to increase the bet by three units because a single-odds game gives us the best chance to make the maximum free-odds bets allowed.

Anytime our pass-line or come bets repeat as wins, our next bet increases by three units. Therefore, our next bet after a win will be six units instead of three, and if it repeats again, it will be raised to nine units, and then to twelve, and so on, as long as the bets continue to repeat and win.

With this kind of increase, after some numbers repeat, you're going to find yourself ahead quite a bit of money. Let's follow a shoot to see how this method works:

Roll	Number	Bets and Results
Come Out	6	$15 on pass line and $25 odds
First Come	11	$15 win
Second Come	8	$15 and $25 odds
Third Come	6	$45 win on pass line 6
		$15 and $25 odds

At this time we're paid off on the 6 and there's a new come-out roll, since 6 was the point and has been made. Because we won our pass-line wager, we now increase our bet on the line to six units, or $30.

New Come Out	5	$30 and $40 odds

At this moment, we have a pass-line and two come numbers established and working for us, so we stop betting.

Next Come	9	No effect on our bets
Next Come	8	$45 win on come 8

The 8 is taken down after it repeats because we had no come bet in the come box, so we have to make a new come wager of six units because the previous bet on this come number was only three units.

Next Come	5	$90 win on point 5
		$30 and $40 odds

There's a new come-out roll because the point was made. At this time we raise our pass-line wager to nine units. After the pass-line bet establishes a number other than 6 or 5, we again stop betting because both numbers have been established as come numbers.

New Come Out	7	$45 win
		$15 loss on come 6
		$30 loss on come 5

The free odds are off on the come-out roll and are returned to us. All our numbers are taken down by the dealer, who removes all the chips on the come bets as losing ones for us.

To summarize our wins and losses at this moment:

Total Wins	$240
Total Losses	$ 45
Net Win	$195

When increasing bets in this manner, you must keep in mind that each bet is treated separately, so that the increase is gradual. Don't be greedy and trust to luck, praying for a hot roll to develop, by socking in heavy money on the layout. With our method, when you're making those big bets, you're in the middle of a hot roll; there's no guesswork here. With this method, you'll be making different bets for different situations on the table. It's fairly easy to follow because when you win any particular bet, you increase only that bet by three units. Don't increase all bets to the highest bet you have on the table, but treat all the bets as separate entities.

In this way, you'll be taking full advantage of a hot roll, at the same time avoiding a situation where you're shoving out more money than you've been taking in.

Greed, as I mentioned, is the danger in craps, as it is in all gambling games. And greed is disguised as anticipation of a hot roll. We don't anticipate anything; we merely go with the dice and take advantage of the roll as it progresses.

What happens when 7 shows on the dice, either as a losing roll by the shooter sevening-out, or as a winning roll on the come out? When the 7 comes up, all our bets revert to the basic three-unit bets. Otherwise, we'll be re-establishing bets at high risk, without taking in any profits ahead of time.

So, remember this cardinal rule: *Whenever a 7 shows on the dice, the bets revert to the basic three units.*

DOUBLE-ODDS GAMES

A number of casinos feature double odds at their craps tables, and these are the choice ones for us. If possible, always play in a double-odds game rather than at a single-odds table. By doing this, you are lowering the house edge and also making more money, since the bulk of your wagers will be on the free-odds bets, with better-than-even-money payoffs after each win.

Instead of betting three units basically, we now bet two units. These can be $2, $10, $50, $200, or any figure divisible by two, which gives us a great range of bets. For example, $20 can be a two-unit bet; as can $40, $60, or $80, and so forth.

No matter what amount you bet, the methods and the principles are the same. It's merely a question of your bankroll and your profit goal.

With double odds, we do exactly the same thing we did with single odds, except that we're betting in two-unit denominations.

• We make a two-unit bet on the pass line.
• After the point is established, we back up the line bet with the maximum amount of chips as a free-odds bet. With

83

double odds, you simply double the pass-line bet when the point or come number is 4, 5, 9, or 10. If the point or come number is a 6 or 8, practically all casinos allowing double odds permit you to bet *five units* behind the line, even though you've bet only two on the line or come bet.

• Make a come bet of two units and give the dealer enough chips to make a maximum free-odds bet on the come number.

• Make a second come bet, and after that number is working for you, stop betting. Intermediate rolls such as 2, 3, 11, or 12 are to be disregarded as far as getting those two come numbers established. If these rolls come up before the two come numbers are working, keep making other come bets.

DOUBLE-ODDS GAMES WITH INCREASED BETS

In increasing our bets in a double-odds game, it's best to increase the wagers by two units after each win, going from two to four, to six, to eight, and so forth as each winning number repeats, either on the pass line or on the come line. This method takes advantage of the five units permitted on the 6 and 8 as point or come numbers, since these numbers come up with the most frequency.

However, you can also increase the bets by one unit and the method will still work for you. One-unit increases are a little more conservative, whereas two-unit increases will really win you a lot of money if you get involved in a hot roll. But the final decision is with you, depending on your temperament and bankroll.

As in the single-odds game, treat each winning bet as a separate entity when raising the bets. For example, if the point number has repeated three times, the bet on the pass line would be eight units. If each come number has repeated only once, each bet would be with only four units.

Betting this way ensures a steady profit when a good roll develops, and doesn't force the issue. Only when numbers repeat, should you increase the bets. Only the greedy losers make maximum wagers, hoping for repeats. We do it the sane way, raising our bets only after the dice show us that a hot roll is in progress.

BASIC METHOD WITH PLACE NUMBERS 6 AND 8

This is a much more aggressive method of betting, which can lead to big profits. This method's one big disadvantage, however, is that it gives the house an edge of 1.52 percent on one or two bets during the betting cycle, instead of the 0.8 percent we give the house when taking single odds, or the lower 0.6 percent when double odds are permitted.

Single Odds

We use the same betting method as in the basic strategy, establishing both a pass-line bet and two come numbers with three units plus the maximum free odds allowed. However, with this new method, we do the following:

If the 6 and/or 8 have not been established as either a pass-line or come bet, then we bet six units on those numbers as place bets.

We don't make the place bets until all our numbers are established and working. The reason we cover the 6 and 8 in this manner is that they are the heart of all hot rolls, and the key numbers in any long shoot. We always prefer to have them as pass-line or come numbers, but that's not always possible. Therefore, with our method we ensure that these numbers are covered.

Let's see how this method works in the course of a shoot:

Roll	Number	Bets and Results
Come Out	5	$15 on pass line and $20 odds
First Come	6	$15 and $25 odds
Second Come	9	$15 and $20 odds

In the basic method, we would stop betting, but here we still have the 8 open, so we hand six chips to the dealer to place $30 on the place-number box 8. Should the 8 come up, we receive $35 in winnings on the place bet, paid off at 7 to 6. The house now has an advantage of 1.52 percent on this bet, but that's the biggest advantage we're going to give them on any wager. We never cover any of the other numbers with place bets.

Once a place number 6 or 8 is covered, it doesn't have to stay as a place bet throughout the roll. For example, if one of the point or come numbers repeats as a winner, and then is taken down, and a new pass-line or come bet establishes the 6 or 8, which is already covered as a place bet, we remove 6 or 8 as a place bet and keep it as a pass line or come number instead. The following roll shows this:

Roll	Number	Bets and Results
Come Out	4	$15 on pass line and $15 odds
First Come	10	$15 and $15 odds
Second Come	9	$15 and $20 odds

Next, we cover the 6 and 8 for $30 apiece as place bets. Since we have two come bets working for us, we stop betting.

Third Come	10	$45 win on come 10

The 10 is taken down as a come number, and we have to make one more come bet.

Fourth Come	6	$35 win as place 6
		$15 and $25 odds

Since we've established the 6 as a come number, we take it down as a place bet. Now we have 4 as the point, 9 and 6 as come numbers, and 8 as a place bet. Since we again have two come numbers working for us, we stop betting.

If the 6 repeats as a come number, it would be taken down, and a new come bet should be made. If the new come number were a 5, for example, then the 6 would be open, and again would be covered as a place bet. If possible, we want the 6 and 8 as points or come numbers, but if that's not the case, we cover them as place bets, but only after the point and two come numbers are working.

Double Odds

This is essentially the same as with single odds. We cover the 6 and/or 8 as place bets after both the point and come numbers have been established, not before both come numbers are working for us.

With double odds, we prefer to have the 6 and 8 as point or come numbers, because we can make a five-unit free-odds bet for every two units we bet on the line or come. But that's not always the case, so we have to content ourselves with the 6 and 8 as place bets.

The only difference between the single- and double-odds games, is that with double odds, the basic bet will be two units, rather than three. Otherwise, using the 6 and 8 as place bets, the same methods are used.

COVERING THE 6 AND 8 AS PLACE NUMBERS WITH INCREASED BETS

This method works equally well for single- and double-odds games. We increase bets the same way on the place numbers 6 and 8, no matter what the casino allows, whether single or double odds.

Here is a quick review of the basic methods with increased bets: With single odds, we increase the line and come-bet units from three to six to nine, by three units after each win.

With double odds, starting with two units, we increase the line and come-bet units by two, from two to four to six to eight after each win.

However, since the place bets on the 6 and 8 are paid off at 7 to 6, it's not possible to increase them in the same terms or units that we increase the underlying line and come bets.

For example, it's not feasible to raise the place bets on the 6 and 8 by three units, or $15, when betting with $5 chips, or to raise them by two units, or $10, when betting with those same $5 chips, because the correct payoff is at 7 to 6 on the 6 and 8 as place numbers, and thus odd amounts would be wagered, which is incorrect. Therefore, when we increase our 6 and 8 place-number bets, the units will be $6 units when making $5 wagers, and $30 units when making $25 bets on line and come numbers.

The increases are as follows: When betting with $5 chips, betting either three or two units on the line and come numbers, either $15 or $10, and then backing up these same numbers with odds, if a place number 6 or 8 is rolled and wins, increase first by *two $6 units*, then, if it wins again, by *three $6 units*. Thereafter, increase by two and then three $6 units, alternating the two and three $6 increasing units.

There's a definite reason for this from a practical viewpoint. If you're at a craps table, and bet $30 on a place number, either 6 or 8, when either number comes up, you are paid $35. That's a common payoff, easily made by a dealer.

However, when you increase that place-number bet to $42 by adding two $6 units to the wager, the new payoff is more difficult to figure out. It amounts to $49, representing seven $6 units paid off at 7 to 6. The next increase will be three more $6 units, now making the bet $60, an easy pay-off of $70 at 7 to 6.

If we simply raised the $6 unit bets by $30 at a time that would make our task much easier, but we avoid doing this because we don't want to lay out too much money on place bets by constantly doubling these bets. If we did so, our third place bet would be $90. We'd rather have it lower, at $60 with our method, and concentrate our biggest wagers on points and come bets at much lower advantages to the house.

On the other hand, if we increased our bets in a definite fixed pattern, for example, either $12 or $18 after each repeat, theoretically, it would be easier, but practically it would create problems because the amounts then put on the place numbers would always give the dealer trouble. The increase is, with two units, from $30 to $42 to $54 to $66. With $18 increases, it goes from $30 to $48 to $66 to $84, all difficult and complicated payoffs.

The payoffs and betting methods become a little more complicated when increasing the place bets, but it's not our fault. It is the casino's—because of their strange payoff at 7 to 6 to ensure an edge over the player on this bet. All the other place-bet payoffs are to $5 and multiples of $5, and any $10 line, come, don't-come, or free-odds bet is easily calculated and paid off, but because of the policy of the casino, a $10 bet on the place number 6 or 8 turns into an unequal wager that cannot be paid off properly.

Let's follow a shoot to see how this all works:

Roll	Number	Bets and Results
Come Out	4	$15 on pass line and $15 odds
First Come	6	$15 and $25 odds
Second Come	9	$15 and $20 odds

We now cover the 8 with a $30 place bet, and stop betting.

      Third Come   8 $35 win on place 8

The place bet is increased to $42.

      Fourth Come   9 $45 win on come 9

There is a new come bet made of $30 because the bet on the 9 was taken down after it won.

Fifth Come	10	$30 and $30 odds
Sixth Come	8	$49 win on place 8

The place bet on the 8 is now increased to $60 by raising it an additional $18.

      Seventh Come   8 $70 win on place 8

The place bet is increased to $72 and the shoot goes on. This kind of roll happens often at the table, and that's the reason we want to cover the 6 and 8 as place bets if they haven't been made as line or come wagers. It can be frustrating to see a 6 or 8 keep coming up without us having a bet on the number on the pass line or come box. The only other way we could cover it is to make continuous come bets, but that creates many risks and puts too much of our money on the layout, subject to a roll of 7 and our losing all the bets.

In betting this method, we should remember that we always prefer the 6 and 8 as point or come numbers rather than as place numbers. There will be times when we already have a place bet out on the 6 and 8, and one of the point or come numbers repeat (numbers other than the 6 and 8) and the next roll of the dice establishes a 6 or 8 as a come number. When this occurs, after we've been paid off on the place bet, we take our place bet down on that number, and are content to have it as a come or point number. For example, suppose the point was 4 and the come numbers were 5 and 10. A 5 repeats, and therefore is taken down as a come number. We make a new come bet. The new number is 6. The 6 has been a place bet and thus was paid off at $35. The 6 is taken down as a place bet, since it's now a come number. Now, we have the point as 4, the come numbers are 6 and 10, and the 8 is covered as a place number. With this method, we don't want to cover all the numbers. We just want to make sure that we have the 6 and 8 working for us one way or another, because, as mentioned before, they are the heart of any potential hot roll, and come up more often on the dice than any of the other numbers.

Let's follow a shoot to see this:

Roll	Number	Bets and Results
Come Out	9	$15 on pass line and $20 odds
First Come	8	$15 and $25 odds
Second Come	10	$15 and $15 odds

We now bet $30 on the place number 6.

Third Come	10	$45 win on come 10

After the win, the 10 is taken down as a come number by the dealer, and so we have to make a new come bet, this time wagering $30 and $30 odds.

Fourth Come	6	$35 win on place 6
		$30 and $50 odds

Since the 6 and 8 are both come numbers, we no longer need the 6 as a place number and we take it down after our $35 win.

Let's continue this same shoot:

Fifth Come	8	$45 win on come 8

The 8 is taken down by the dealer and we make a new come bet of $30.

| Sixth Come | 6 | $90 win on come 6 |
| | | $30 and $50 odds |

The 8 is now open. Instead of betting it at $30, you can bet it more aggressively at $42, counting its repeat as a come number as a place-bet repeat. Or you can be more conservative and place it at $30. Either way is fine. Let's be more aggressive here. The 8 is now bet as a place number at $42.

| Seventh Come | 8 | $49 win on place 8 |

The 8 is now raised to $60 as a place bet, and the shoot goes on. A few more repeats and a few more numbers coming up and you will be taking in a small fortune on this roll, which began with $15 basic bets. Let's follow this shoot to its very end.

| Eighth Come | 12 | No effect on our bets |

Having two come numbers, the 10 and the 6 established, we stop betting.

| Ninth Come | 10 | $90 win on come 10 |

We make another come bet of $45 since the 10 was taken down as a come number by the dealer.

| Tenth Come | 4 | $45 and $45 odds |
| Eleventh Come | 8 | $70 win on place 8 |

The 8 as a place bet is raised to $72.

| Twelfth Come | 3 | No effect on our bets |
| Thirteenth Come | 4 | $135 win on come 4 |

The 4 is taken down as a come bet by the dealer, and our next come bet is $60.

Fourteenth Come	9	$45 win on point 9
		$60 and $60 odds

Finally, the point 9 was made by the shooter, and there's a new come-out roll. We now wager $30 on the pass line, because our previous pass-line wager was only $15.

New Come Out	7	$30 win on pass line
		$30 loss on come 6
		$60 loss on come 9

We didn't lose any of the free-odds bets because they were off on the come-out roll, and we didn't lose our $72 bet on the 8 as a place number because place bets are also off on the come-out roll. Let's summarize our wins and losses on this good roll:

Total Wins	$634
Total Losses	$ 90
Net Win	$544

It was a good win for us, since we started out with only $15 basic bets and worked our bets up as the roll developed.

That, in essence, is the method of betting using the place 6 and 8 bets, and increasing our bets not only on the line and come wagers but also on the place bets. This method is slightly more risky because we're giving the house a 1.52 percent edge on the place bets, but it has the advantage of keeping the 6 and 8 covered as betting numbers and, with a moderately good roll, a lot of money can be made.

XI

WINNING METHODS OF PLAY: WRONG BETTORS

Unlike right bettors, whose best strategy changes according to the table they're at, permitting either single or double odds, the wrong bettor uses the same betting method at either kind of game. This is so because we don't recommend laying double free odds when betting wrong.

We realize that double odds cuts the house advantage from 0.8 percent to 0.6 percent, but we're *laying* odds, not taking them, and one bad run of the dice will wipe out our bankroll if the numbers repeat while we're laying those full double odds.

For instance, if the point is 4 or 10, a $10 line bet forces us to lay $40 in double odds. If a few of these numbers repeat, we could be in real trouble and out of the game, risking our money on double odds against the numbers, when, if we had bet only single odds, we would still have some of our bankroll intact. So, for purposes of our method, all odds laid will be single odds. The extra 0.2 percent won't make that much difference to us in the long run.

Why, then, have we suggested double odds when betting right? We have a whole other ballgame in that situation. We were taking odds, not laying them, and a $10 line bet on a 4 or 10 requires only a $20 odds wager at double odds, which, when won, pays off $40 for that $20. However, when betting wrong, our $40 free-odds bet nets us only $20.

When using our basic method, we'll be betting at least $5 on each situation, whether it's don't pass or don't come, so that we can lay single odds correctly no matter what the point or come number. The following are the odds laid on wrong bets against the various numbers:

Number	Correct Odds Against
4 and 10	2 to 1
5 and 9	3 to 2
6 and 8	6 to 5

When you bet $5 on don't pass or don't come, all casinos allow you to lay $9 at 9 to 6 where the point or come number is 5 or 9. This extra amount is allowed because most casinos don't pay off in half-dollars at their crap tables, and the correct bet would be at 7½ to 5 against the 5 or 9, which can't be done.

All our examples will deal with a $10 wager, which is the easiest to explain in terms of odds and the easiest to follow. With a $10 bet, we lay $12 for $10 against the 6 or 8, $15 for $10 against the 5 or 9, and $20 for $10 against the 4 or 10.

However, a wrong bettor need not bet in such small amounts if the player can afford to make heavier wagers or wants to go after a bigger profit. But, if the player bets with one $25 chip, there will be problems when the point or come is 5 or 9, since a $30 free-odds bet nets only $20, less than the original bet on the line or don't come. To lay the correct bet, the wrong bettor must lay $39 to net $26, which gets complicated. Some casinos might allow the wrong wager $45 to net $30, but an easier way to bet wrong in these amounts is to bet $30, not $25, on line and don't-come wagers. In this way all payoffs can be simply calculated.

Players betting wrong need not be stuck with $30, however. They can bet $40, $50, $60, or higher amounts, just as long as the bets are in even amounts. There's enough to keep track of and worry about at a craps table without the added pressure of figuring out exact odds bets. That's why we recommend betting in these gradations, to make everything simple.

WRONG BETTORS: THE BASIC METHOD

Here's how this method works. It's a little different from the basic method for right bettors because we have certain safeguards built in. These safeguards protect us from the one danger of wrong bettors: a hot roll that completely ruins us. We take this factor into consideration and stop ourselves out, to use a stock market expression, when the numbers start repeating.

In other words, when the roll gets hot and the numbers coming up give us losses, we automatically stop betting and pull away for a while.

• We make a don't-pass bet of any amount we care to, then we lay single odds after the point is established.

• We make a don't-come bet, and lay single odds after the don't-come number is established. This don't-come wager should be in the same amount as the don't-pass bet.

• We make another don't-come wager in the same amount as our don't-pass bet, and after that number is established, we stop betting.

If a 2, 3, 11, or 12 is rolled during the time we are trying to establish our two don't-come wagers, we either collect or lose or have a standoff on these numbers and keep making don't-come wagers.

However, in certain situations, there may be complications and it is for these situations that we've structured our safeguards. The safeguards are as follows:

• If, before two don't-come bets are established, the point is made, we make only one other don't-pass bet. If that don't-pass or a don't-come bet is lost by a repeating number, we stop betting until the shooter sevens-out, and we patiently wait for that to happen, no matter how long it takes.

• If, before two don't-come numbers are established, one of the don't-come numbers repeats, we make another don't-come wager. Any other repeating number leading to a loss on either the don't-pass line or don't come stops us from betting until the shooter sevens-out. In other words, after one repeating number, we continue betting, trying to establish both don't-come numbers after the don't-pass number, but any other repeat stops us from making any other wagers.

• If the don't-pass and don't-come numbers are established without any repeats, if either the don't-pass or don't-come number repeats, we make one other wager on either don't pass or don't come, whichever has repeated. We make no further wagers then, until the shooter sevens-out.

The purpose of this safeguard is to protect the wrong bettors from the one thing they fear the most, and that is a hot roll that will really hurt them.

Once we stop betting due to this safeguard, whether it's for ten minutes or an hour, we wait for the shooter to seven-out. We must be patient. We never fight the dice when betting wrong.

We thus avoid the downfall of all wrong bettors, being wiped out by a hot roll while fighting it. As our numbers repeat after they've been established, we're out of the betting until a new shooter comes out.

There is no deviation from this safeguard. We're not interested in hunches or feelings here. We're interested in the facts and the plain truth, which is that a hot roll is in progress, one we can't control and one that is dangerous for wrong bettors.

If the roll goes on and on, and all your numbers have been wiped out by repeats, you don't have to hang around the table, watching. You can go to another table, one that will probably be a lot colder than the one you just left. A cold table, with few numbers or points repeating, is ideal territory for a wrong bettor.

Another reason we stress this safeguard is this: It will be your experience as a wrong bettor, following our methods, that you'll win a lot of small bets, and will have a number of small wins, while the right bettors are experiencing a lot of small losses. They're waiting for the hot roll to get them going on a winning streak, while you want to get away from any long betting losses during that hot streak.

Examples of several shoots will demonstrate our betting methods and its safeguards: For purposes of these shoots, you'll be a $10 bettor on both don't pass and don't come, laying single odds.

Roll	*Number*	*Bets and Results*
Come Out	5	$10 on don't pass and $15 odds
First Come	12	Standoff
Second Come	6	$10 and $12 odds
Third Come	11	$10 loss
Fourth Come	3	$10 win
Fifth Come	10	$10 and $20 odds

This is the basic betting method in operation. We disregard the intermediate rolls of 12, 11, and 3 in establishing our two don't-come bets. At this time we stop betting.

Sixth Come	8	No effect on our bets
Seventh Come	6	$22 loss on 6

The 6 has been taken down by the dealer and so we make another don't-come bet. This is our final wager until the shooter sevens-out.

Eighth Come	6	$10 and $12 odds
Ninth Come	7	$20 win on point 5
		$20 win on 10
		$20 win on 6

98

The above shoot netted us $38 in winnings, because the 7 showed up, winning all our previous don't-pass and don't-come wagers. It's the one number we want to see on the dice, and the one the right bettors fear the most.

Let's follow another shoot to show our safeguards in action:

Roll	*Number*	*Bets and Results*
Come Out	8	$10 on don't pass and $12 odds
First Come	6	$10 and $12 odds
Second Come	8	$22 loss on point 8
		$10 and $12 odds

There is now a new come-out and we make another don't-pass bet.

New Come Out	9	$10 on don't pass and $15 odds

At this time we've established our don't-pass number and two don't-come numbers, so we stop betting. No matter what happens, we don't bet again until the shooter sevens-out, for we don't want to lose more than one repeating number to a fresh bet.

We're taking no chances with this betting method, but it's a great one for making money at the tables. The casinos dislike players who bet this way, for they leave themselves in the best possible position, taking in small wins, but never hanging around, making losing bet after losing bet as the numbers repeat over and over again.

Often, when at a cold table, I've seen the few wrong bettors make money steadily while all the right bettors keep losing, then, when a hot roll came up, to my dismay, I watched the wrong bettors lose everything they had previously won fighting the dice.

You can't make money going against the cubes, especially if you're a wrong bettor, because those repeats will kill your bankroll. You're always laying odds and those losses can mount if you're stubbornly hoping the dice will turn. They won't do anything just because you're hoping they will, and so you must make intelligent bets and never, never fight the dice. Our safeguards with this betting method prevent you from losing everything during a hot roll.

WRONG BETTORS: BASIC METHODS WITH INCREASED BETS

Before going into the new method, let's review the basic method to make certain we understand it fully, including the safeguards.

• We make a don't-pass bet and lay single odds after the point is established.

• We make a don't-come bet in the same amount, and lay single odds against the don't-come number that's been established.

• We make another don't-come bet in the same amount as the don't-pass wager, and lay single odds against that don't-come number once it's been established.

Tied up with this betting method is the safeguard, which can be stated as follows:

If we've lost a bet, either don't pass or don't come, by a number repeating, we make another bet, either don't pass or don't come (whichever has repeated). If we have another number repeat and lose for us, whether don't pass or don't come, we stop betting until the shooter sevens-out, no matter how long that might take.

To illustrate our method using increased bets after every win, we're going to use a basic $10 bet to begin with. However, you are free to use whatever size bet desired, depending on your bankroll and profit goal, but to make things easier, your bets should be in even amounts, such as $10, $20, $30, $50, $100, and so on. With odd amounts being bet, such as $25 or $35, it is difficult to figure out the maximum free odds permitted with single odds.

With all our wrong betting methods, we will lay only single odds in order to protect our bankroll from one bad run of the dice.

The increased bets in our betting method for wrong players will occur after a shooter sevens-out, when all the don't-pass and don't-come wagers win at one time.

For players who start with $5 bets on don't pass, we'd suggest they increase their bets by one unit of $5 at a time. For other players, we suggest a unit increase of two units after each win, although this is not mandatory. Some players feel more comfortable, if they're $10 players, betting $5 more after each win, rather than $10. The method works just as well that way, but it is our experience that the dice run in streaks, and sometimes the perfect cold streak lasts a very long time, and it is during these cold runs, when the shooters continually seven-out after a couple of rolls, that the wrong bettor makes the most money.

For purposes of our betting methods, the player will increase the bet after each win by two units. If a $10 bettor, the next bet will be $20, and then $30, and so forth. A player starting with $30 will increase it to $40 and then $50 and so forth. A player with a large bankroll who can make a $50 don't-pass bet to start off with is betting two $25 units at the outset.

Therefore, an increase by two units after each win, or $50 at a time, is possible. If the bettor is not comfortable with this, he or she can increase the bet by $20 or $30 after each win, not by $25, which might create difficulties in betting against the 5 and 9 as point or don't-come numbers.

No matter what increases the wrong bettor feels comfortable with, the player should continually increase the wagers after each win to maximize profits when the dice are cold.

We'll show our shoot with a $10 bettor making one don't-pass and two don't-come wagers, laying single odds. After

a shooter sevens-out, the increase will be by two units to
$20, and then all subsequent don't-come bets will also be
increased to $20. The don't-come bet, to refresh our mem-
ory, is always the same unit bet as the don't-pass wager.

Roll	Number	Bets and Results
Come Out	5	$10 on don't pass and $15 odds
First Come	6	$10 and $12 odds
Second Come	7	$10 loss on don't come bet
		$20 win on point 5
		$20 win on 6
Total Wins		$40
Total Losses		$10
Net Win		$30

This is a fairly common type of roll at the craps table,
and it drives the right bettors up the wall, because 7 shows
up before any numbers repeat. However, for wrong bettors,
this kind of stunted shoot is perfect.

Having won our previous bets when the shooter sevens-
out, we now increase our wagers by two units, to $20. A
new shooter picks up the dice and prepares to roll them as
we make our $20 don't-pass wager.

Roll	Number	Bets and Results
Come Out	8	$20 on don't pass and $24 odds
First Come	9	$20 and $30 odds
Second Come	3	$20 win
Third Come	7	$20 loss
		$40 win on point 8
		$40 win on 9
Total Wins		$100
Total Losses		$ 20
Net Win		$ 80

The dice are still ice cold, so we continue to raise our bets by two units. Our new don't-pass bet will be $30 as the new shooter selects the dice and is about to begin the first roll.

Roll	Number	Bets and Results
Come Out	12	Standoff
New Come Out	4	$30 on don't pass and $60 odds
First Come	5	$30 and $45 odds
Second Come	10	$30 and $60 odds
Third Come	6	No effect on our bets
Fourth Come	8	No effect on our bets
Fifth Come	8	No effect on our bets
Sixth Come	6	No effect on our bets
Seventh Come	7	$60 win on point 4
		$60 win on 5
		$60 win on 10
Total Wins		$180
Total Losses		$ 0
Net Win		$180

Watching the 6s and 8s repeat, we see why we have to limit ourselves to two don't-come numbers. The more numbers we establish, the more targets we set out for repeats and losses.

No shooter has yet made a point, so we continue to increase our bet on the don't-pass line, this time increasing by two units to $40.

Roll	Number	Bets and Results
Come Out	4	$40 on don't pass and $80 odds
First Come	11	$40 loss
Second Come	6	$40 and $48 odds
Third Come	2	$40 win
Fourth Come	8	$40 and $48 odds
Fifth Come	3	No effect on our bets
Sixth Come	6	$88 loss on 6

The 6 is taken down as a don't-come number and we make another $40 bet on don't come. We stop betting until the shooter sevens-out, if another don't-come number is established.

Seventh Come	5	$40 and $60 odds
Eighth Come	7	$80 win on point 4
		$80 win on 8
		$80 win on 5
Total Wins	$280	
Total Losses	$128	
Net Win	$152	

A new shooter is examining the dice, ready to throw them, and so we bet $50 in the don't-pass betting area.

Roll	Number	Bets and Results
Come Out	9	$50 on don't pass and $75 odds
First Come	5	$50 and $75 odds
Second Come	10	$50 and $100 odds
Third Come	9	$125 loss on point 9

There's now a new come-out roll with the same shooter holding the dice, since he made his point. We now bet the same $50 on the don't pass.

New Come Out	3	$50 win
New Come Out	7	$50 loss
		$100 win on 5
		$100 win on 10
Total Wins	$250	
Total Losses	$175	
Net Win	$ 75	

Although the shooter didn't seven-out, the 7 coming up on the come-out roll was a loser for us, and now, if we increase our bets to $60 on don't pass, we'll be risking all our previous wins trying to establish a don't-pass and don't-come number.

We can do one of two things: We can reduce our bets to the basic two units, starting all over again, or we can walk away from the table, having taken advantage of a long, cold roll.

At this time we can count our total wins and losses to see how well we've made out during these shoots.

Total Wins	$850
Total Losses	$333
Net Win	$517

An aggressive player might make the $60 bets, trying to make a real killing while holding the casino's money as profits. A more conservative player might want to lock up the profits by reducing the next wager to two units or leaving the table altogether. No matter what is done, the win has been a good one, due to the increased bets after each shooter sevened-out.

XII

MONEY MANAGEMENT

Before we even discuss the amount of money necessary to play the game of casino craps properly, we're going to state that *no one should ever gamble with money they can't afford to lose.* If money is needed for necessities such as rent, food, clothing, medical and educational expenses, it shouldn't be risked at any game of chance.

Therefore, never play casino craps with money that would hurt you if you lost it. Only play with money you can spare for gambling purposes. And when you play with spare money, make sure it isn't "scared money" or insufficient funds for the game you're going to play. This subject is covered in the section on the bankroll needed for one session of play contained in this chapter.

The main aspects of money management are as follows:
* Money needed for one session of play
* Loss limits for any single session of play
* Wins and how to handle them
* Money needed for an extended period of play
We'll cover these topics one at a time.

MONEY NEEDED FOR ONE SESSION OF PLAY

Right Bettors

To decide on the amount of money that's necessary for any single session of play, we take into consideration our basic betting methods.

A right bettor will be making a pass-line wager, taking single or double odds, then will be making two come bets, getting both come numbers established, also with free odds, either single or double. When wagering at a single-odds table, this player will bet three units and then maximum single odds; at a double-odds table, two units and double odds on each wager.

If the player bets with $15 as the basic wager, for each cycle of betting necessary to establish the point number and two come numbers, he or she needs approximately $100. If the right bettor is betting $10 at a double-odds table as the basic wager, approximately $100 will establish the same numbers. Therefore, a right bettor using our methods and betting with $5 chips needs approximately seven to ten times that one complete cycle as a single-session bankroll. Seven times is our suggested minimum bankroll, and ten times our suggested maximum bankroll for each single session. This would enable the player to overcome any temporary bad streaks at the table where the dice are running cold, and would enable him or her to take advantage of that hot roll when it finally arrives.

So, if you want to use our basic betting methods, you must bring from $700 to $1,000 to a table, if your basic bet is $15 with single odds, or $10 with double odds.

If you're following the same basic betting methods, but are limiting yourself to a $5 basic wager with either single or double odds, then you'll need much less. In this case, a complete betting cycle will cost you at least $30 at a single-odds table, and about $45 at a double-odds table. Therefore, you should have between $210 and $300 for the single-odds game, and between $300 and $450 for the double-odds game. These figures are sane ones, neither conservative nor reckless, and will enable you to have a lot of action at a craps table, and allow you to be around for the favorable rolls when they occur.

On the other hand, if you bring a fixed amount of cash to a table, you might ask, "What betting limits can I afford with this money?" For example, if you take $100 to a table, your basic bet should be only $2, not more, for a $5 table will be too rich for you and you'll end up betting with insufficient or "scared" money.

If you bring $200, you should be betting at a $5 table with single odds only. A bankroll of $300 will put you at the minimum end of a $5 table with double odds. If you have $500, a common amount brought to a table by many gamblers, then you should bet only $10 as a basic wager at a single-odds game.

Follow these guidelines closely. You can't always win at a craps table, nor are you able to determine what the dice are going to do. You may start off badly at the table and begin your session with heavy losses. Then you'll be thankful that you have enough in reserve to weather the storm until the dice turn in your favor.

Wrong Bettors

When betting wrong, if you use a $5 basic bet on don't pass, then lay single odds, and make two don't-come bets of $5 each, again with single odds, you'll need about $40 for each full betting cycle.

To have enough for a single session of play, you should have between seven and ten times that amount with you, or between $280 and $400, the minimum and maximum limits.

A $10 bettor, using our methods of wagering and play, would require $80 for a complete cycle of play, and thus between $560 and $800 in reserve. With don't bettors, because one roll of a 7 doesn't destroy all the previously established bets, the minimum would be sufficient. Therefore, you can bring $300 to the table for a basic $5 bet with two don't-come wagers as well, and $600 to the game for your $10 bets with two don't-come wagers.

What if you have only $200? It doesn't really pay to bet less than $5 on don't pass and don't come because you will deprive yourself of laying odds against the 6 and 8, so you would have to limit yourself to one don't-pass and one additional don't-come wager, instead of two don't-come wagers as suggested in our basic method. This will be all right, although it is a bit conservative.

In any event, follow our guidelines: They've been tested under actual game conditions and have made a number of players winners when betting wrong.

LOSS LIMITS: SINGLE SESSION

Players should *never* lose more than what they have brought to the table. Never! And they should never reach into their pockets for more cash after they have lost their single-session money. When you've lost it all, as will sometimes happen, leave the table and accept your loss. You'll make it up another time, but there's nothing worse than being at a table that's unfavorable for you. The tide doesn't have to turn in your favor just because you bring out more money.

If you're down to a few chips and you don't have enough for another betting cycle, forcing you to take money out of your pocket, leave the table at this time. Don't ever put yourself in the position of reaching into your wallet for more cash.

For example, you need approximately $100 to complete a cycle as a right bettor, wagering $15 on pass line and two come bets and taking maximum single odds. If you have only $70 left, don't start making bets. Leave the game. Preserve your $70 for another table and another session, which has to be better for you.

WINS AND HOW TO HANDLE THEM

A right bettor who gets a hot roll should leave after that hot roll is over, no matter how he or she is doing. Generally, if the player followed our methods of betting, that hot roll will make a lot of money. But after it's over, the player should get away, because it's our experience that only one hot roll comes to each table during the time a player is there.

If there's been no really hot roll, but the dice have been good to you and you're winning, then endeavor to double your original bankroll at the table. If this can't be done, then try and put aside about forty to sixty units that you have won together with your original bankroll, and leave with this as your winnings.

In other words, don't be greedy. If you've locked up this money, leave with profits. Suppose you're winning about ninety units and you brought one hundred to the table. You haven't quite doubled your money, but if you put away fifty of those units as profits and play with the rest, you might win even more. If you lose the rest, and are down to your fifty winning units, get away from the table a winner.

You can either paint a mental profit picture for yourself or move the chips in the rail to one side as your profits. Better still, put them in your pocket and train yourself never to reach for cash or chips locked away out of sight.

MONEY NEEDED FOR AN EXTENDED PERIOD OF PLAY

More often than not, if you gamble, you won't limit yourself to just one session of play and then stop. You'll probably be playing for the day, for the weekend, or longer. In that case, you need more than just enough money for one session of gambling, and if you want to have a sufficient bankroll, you should follow the guidelines set forth.

• For one day's play, take five times your single-session bankroll. If you need $700 for one session of craps, bring along $3,500.

• For a weekend of play, take between seven and ten times your single-session bankroll. Seven should get you through the weekend, overcoming the worst possible luck, but ten is a little safer.

• For a longer stay, take along ten times the single-session bankroll. This may seem like a lot of money, but you're going to do a lot of gambling, and your luck may be bad for a while. With this kind of reserve, you should have enough for the good runs, when you'll be able to win it back in spades.

This is not to say you should expect to lose. Using our betting methods is the sanest and safest way to play the game of casino craps, and you should end up a winner. But temporary losses do occur and you must be prepared for them. No one wins all the time and, conversely, no one loses all the time. With our methods, your wins should be big and your losses small.

A Complete Table of Odds and Casino Advantage

Bet	Casino Payoff	Percentage of Casino Advantage
Pass Line	Even money	1.41
With Single Odds	Even money plus odds	0.8
With Double Odds	Even money plus odds	0.6
Come	Even money	1.41
With Single Odds	Even money plus odds	0.8
With Double Odds	Even money plus odds	0.6
Don't Pass	Even money	1.4
With Single Odds	Even money plus odds	0.8
With Double Odds	Even money plus odds	0.6
Don't Come	Even money	1.4
With Single Odds	Even money plus odds	0.8
With Double Odds	Even money plus odds	0.6
Place Bets		
4 or 10	9 to 5	6.67
5 or 9	7 to 5	4.0
6 or 8	7 to 6	1.52
Buy Bet		
4 or 10	2 to 1 (less 5% commission)	4.76
Lay Wagers (all with 5% commission)		
4 or 10	1 to 2	2.44
5 or 9	2 to 3	3.23
6 or 8	5 to 6	4.0
Big Six and Big Eight	Even money	9.09

A Complete Table of Odds and Casino Advantage

Field Bet

2 and 12 at 2 to 1	Even money except for 2 and 12	5.55
2 or 12 at 3 to 1	Even money except for 2 and 12	2.7

CENTER WAGERS

Bet	True Odds	Casino Payoff	Casino Advantage
Any 7	5 to 1	4 to 1	16.67%
Any Craps	8 to 1	7 to 1	11.1%
2 or 12	35 to 1	30 to 1	13.89%
		30 for 1	16.67%
3 or 11	17 to 1	15 to 1	11.1%
		15 for 1	16.67%
Hardways			
4 or 10	8 to 1	7 to 1	11.1%
6 or 8	10 to 1	9 to 1	9.09%

GLOSSARY OF CASINO CRAPS TERMS

Advantage; Casino advantage The superior position the casino has over the player in terms of odds on any particular bet, often expressed as a percentage (%). Also known as **Edge** or *vigorish*.

Any craps A one-roll center bet determined by the next roll of the dice, which the player bets will come up 2, 3, or 12.

Any seven A one-roll center bet that the next throw of the dice will come up 7.

Back line A wager on either the don't pass or don't come.

Bar the 12 A term found on the layout in both the don't-pass and don't-come betting areas, making the roll of 12 a standoff between the wrong bettor and the casino. In some casinos the 2 is barred instead of the 12.

Betting right Wagering that the dice will pass, or win. See also **Pass-line bet**.

Betting wrong Betting that the dice will not pass, that they will lose. See also **Don't-pass bet**.

Big Six and Big Eight A wager found on the layout, paying even money. By making this bet, the player is wagering that either the 6 or 8, or both, will come up before a 7 is rolled.

Boxman The casino executive in charge of a particular craps table. He is seated at the table between the two standing dealers.

Bring out A term used commonly by stickmen when exhorting players to make certain bets in order to have the number rolled. "Bet on the hard 10; bring it out."

Buck See **Marker puck**.

Buy the 4 and 10 A player, by paying the casino a 5 percent commission, can buy, rather than make a place bet, on these two numbers and be paid off at the correct odds.

Casino checks See **Chips**.

Change color A term for the changing of casino chips into larger or smaller denominations.

Chips The tokens issued by the casino in place of cash, having an equivalent value, which are used for betting purposes by the players. Also known as **Casino checks**.

Cold dice A roll or rolls where the dice aren't passing or winning.

Come bet A wager that the dice will pass, which can only be made after the come-out roll.

Come box The layout space designated for a come bet.

Come-out roll Any roll made before a point is established.

Craps 1. The name of the game. 2. The roll of a 2, 3, or 12.

Craps out Shooter rolls a 2, 3, or 12 on the come-out roll.

Crew The four dealers who work together at a craps table.

Dealer A casino employee who wears the uniform of the casino and works directly with the players either as a standing dealer or as a stickman.

Dice A pair of cubes, each with six sides, numbered from 1 to 6 by the use of dots, which, when rolled by a shooter, determine all payoffs and collections in casino craps.

Die The singular for dice; a single cube.

Disk See **Marker puck**.

Don't-come bet A bet made after the come-out roll against the dice passing.

Don't-come box The layout space designated for don't-come wagers.

Don't-pass bet A wager against the dice made on the come-out roll only.

Don't-pass line The layout space designated for don't-pass wagers.

Double-odds bet A free-odds bet made at double the original bet for right bettors, and double the original payoff for wrong bettors.

Easy; easy way The roll of a 4, 6, 8, or 10 other than as a pair. A 1–3 is an "easy" 4.

Edge See **Advantage**.

Even money Any payoff made at 1 to 1.

Field bet A one-roll wager made that the next roll of the dice will be either a 2, 3, 4, 9, 10, 11, or 12.

Floorman A casino executive who stands in the craps pit overseeing one or more craps tables.

Free-odds bet A wager made in addition to a line, come, or don't-come bet, paid off at correct odds.

Front line Another term used to designate the **Pass line**.

Hardway bet A wager made on either the 4, 6, 8, or 10 that these numbers will be rolled as a pair before they are thrown as an easy number, or before 7 shows on the dice.

Hop bet A one-roll bet on any number the player selects, usually made at disadvantageous odds.

Horn bet A one-roll bet combining the 2, 3, 11, and 12.

Hot roll A series of throws where points and numbers constantly come up for a long period of time.

Inside numbers The place numbers 5, 6, 8, and 9.

Lay wager A bet made by a wrong bettor against the numbers coming up, for which a 5 percent commission is paid.

Layout The imprinted felt surface of the craps table, showing the wagers that can be made by the players, with appropriate spaces for these bets.

Marker puck A round plastic object under the control of each standing dealer. One side is white and the other black, and it is used to designate whether or not there is a come-out roll. Also called disk or buck.

Nickels The common casino term for $5 chips.

Odds bets See **Free-odds bet**.

Off A term designating that certain bets are not working on the come-out roll. Also, an oral instruction by a player that particular bets, such as place bets, are not working during certain rolls of the dice.

On base The term for a standing dealer.

One-roll bets Wagers won or lost by the next roll of the dice.

On the stick The term designating that a dealer is a stickman.

Outside numbers The place numbers 4, 5, 9, and 10.

Parlay See **Press; press a bet.**

Pass A winning decision for the dice.

Pass line The layout space designated for pass-line bets.

Pass-line bet A wager by a right bettor that the dice will win.

Payoff Chips given to a winning player.

Pit boss The casino executive in charge of all the craps tables making up a craps pit.

Place bets; place numbers A bet made on the numbers 4, 5, 6, 8, 9, and 10 in the place boxes, that these numbers either singly or in combination will come up before 7 is rolled.

Player A bettor.

Point Any of the following numbers, 4, 5, 6, 8, 9, or 10, thrown on the come-out roll, which number has to be repeated before a 7 is rolled for the pass-line players to win their bets.

Press; press a bet To increase a previous bet, usually by doubling it.

Proposition bets Wagers that can be made in the center of the layout.

Quarters The slang casino term for $25 chips.

Rails The grooved area around the craps table where players can keep chips not in play.

Right bettor A craps player betting that the dice will pass.

Roll A single throw of the dice. Also, a complete cycle or series of throws of the dice until the shooter sevens-out.

Seven-out To roll a 7 after a point has been established, losing both the pass-line bet and the dice.

Shoot The designation of a complete series of rolls ending when the shooter holding the dice sevens-out.

Shooter The player at the table who is rolling the dice.

Single-odds bets A free-odds bet equal to the original bet for right bettors and equal to the payoff for wrong bettors.

Stickman A dealer who calls the game and controls the dice with a flexible stick.

Take down To remove a bet from the layout.

Tip A gratuity given to the dealers by the players. Also known as **Toke**.

Toke See **Tip**.

Working The designation that bets made are subject to the next roll of the dice. Bets are said to be "on" when working.

Wrong bettor A bettor who wagers against the dice passing, who bets that they will lose.

Yo-leven The common slang term used by stickmen to designate the roll of an 11.